THE
HIDDEN
ELEPHANT

THE
HIDDEN ELEPHANT

Alyosha Ryabinov

Copyright © 2024 by
Alyosha Ryabinov

All rights reserved.
This book, or parts thereof,
may not be reproduced
in any form without permission.

Paperback ISBN: 978-1-63337-811-7
E-Book ISBN: 978-1-63337-812-4

Printed in the United States of America
1 3 5 7 9 10 8 6 4 2

I want to express special thanks to Alex Wolf for transcribing the text from spoken messages and to my daughter, Yasmine, for designing the book cover as well as those who helped edit it and chose to be anonymous.

Dedicated to my loving wife, Jody, for her support and encouragement, as well as taking many duties upon herself to give me time to complete this book. I also want to dedicate this book to my children, Josiah and Yasmine, as well as to all our grandchildren: the existing ones and those who are yet to come.

Table of Contents

Introduction		...i
Chapter 1	The Kingdom on Earth	...1
Chapter 2	Four Messages of the Gospel of the Kingdom According to Isaiah	...15
Chapter 3	Good and Evil	...19
Chapter 4	Lech Lecha	...27
Chapter 5	Nimrod	...31
Chapter 6	The Hidden Elephant	...37
Chapter 7	The Children of Eber	...47
Chapter 8	Abraham and Ruth	...53
Chapter 9	Ruth	...63
Chapter 10	Salvation	...79
Chapter 11	Shalom	...87
Chapter 12	The Hidden Kingdom in the Scroll of Esther	...97
Chapter 13	Judah	...109
Chapter 14	The Elephant Out of Hiding	...117

Introduction

Every Shabbat and on Appointed Times (*Moedim*) in most synagogues around the world these words are recited:

וְהָיָה יְהוָה לְמֶלֶךְ, עַל-כָּל-הָאָרֶץ; בַּיּוֹם הַהוּא, יִהְיֶה יְהוָה אֶחָד--וּשְׁמוֹ אֶחָד

And the LORD shall be King over all the earth; in that day shall the LORD be One, and His name one. (Zechariah 14:9 JPS)

This prophecy tells us our present age will end, and the world to come will begin with God reigning as the King over the entire earth. Gloriously, the goal of the Holy Scriptures, both the Tanakh (the Old Covenant) and Brit haHadasha (the New Covenant) is to relate to humankind the main intent of God, which is to rule over the entire earth.

> God has gone up with a shout,
> The Lord with the sound of a trumpet.
> Sing praises to God, sing praises!
> Sing praises to our King, sing praises!
> For God is the King of all the earth;
> Sing praises with understanding.
> God reigns over the nations;

> God sits on His holy throne.
> The princes of the people have gathered together,
> The people of the God of Abraham.
> For the shields of the earth belong to God;
> He is greatly exalted. (Psalm 47:5-9 NKJ)

This Psalm prophetically speaks about God's coming and reigning over the Earth.

For hundreds of years Christians have been preaching what is called the gospel of salvation in spite of the fact that the term "gospel of salvation" appears only one time in the entire Bible: in Ephesians 1:13. It also appears as the gospel of peace (Ephesians 6:15), and the gospel of God (Romans 1:1). But the real focus of the Holy Scriptures is the gospel of the kingdom. And the meaning of the "gospel of the kingdom" is not exactly the same as the "gospel of salvation."

The message of salvation is only a part of the message of the kingdom. In this book we will learn that the message of the kingdom of God has four areas, and salvation is only one them. Without understanding God's purposes for Israel, it is impossible to understand the fullness of the message of the kingdom of God. You see, if God's designs only concern salvation, then there is no need for Israel. But the message of the kingdom of God without Israel is a "replacement kingdom message." One of the major purposes of this book is to show that the message of the kingdom is not possible without Israel. Sadly, the majority of the body of Yeshua today still believes in replacement theology. They see no purpose for the restoration of Israel and Jerusalem.

INTRODUCTION

Theologies like dominion theology, some versions of seven mountains theology, and others have totally replaced Israel. Instead, God's promises to Israel are now being attributed to "the church." But the establishment of the kingdom of God, where Israel and Jerusalem play a vital role, is like the hidden elephant that most people do not see in spite of the fact that it is so obvious from Genesis to Revelation. For example, the entire book of the prophet Zechariah focuses on Jerusalem. Even when the Lord rebukes Satan in Zechariah chapter 3, the prophet states, "The Lord *who has chosen Jerusalem* rebuke you!" (Zechariah 3:2). Why not just say: "The Lord rebuke you"? It is because Jerusalem is so important to God, which one day will be the center for His presence and His glory. When the Lord returns, Jerusalem will become the capital of the kingdom of God on Earth.

> Thus says the Lord: "I will return to Zion, and dwell in the midst of Jerusalem. Jerusalem shall be called the City of Truth, the Mountain of the Lord of hosts, the Holy Mountain." (Zechariah 8:3)

It is my deep conviction that only within the context of the kingdom can we find our true identities and then our purpose in being co-builders with God of His wonderful kingdom on Earth.

1
The Kingdom on Earth

What was the message of Yeshua during his time on the Earth? Consider these key passages:

> From that time Jesus (Yeshua) began to preach and to say, "Repent, for the *kingdom of heaven is at hand.*" (Mat 4:17 NKJ)

> And Jesus went about all Galilee, teaching in their synagogues, preaching the *gospel of the kingdom,*[1] and healing all kinds of sickness and all kinds of disease among the people. (Mat 4:23 NKJ)

> … but He (Yeshua) said to them, "I must preach *the kingdom of God* to the other cities also, because *for this purpose* I have been sent." (Luke 4:43 NKJ)

And, of course, here is the well-known line from the Lord's Prayer:

> "…Your kingdom come, Your will be done on earth as it is in heaven." (Matt 6:10 NKJ)

---

[1] All italics in verses are author's for emphasis.

According to Luke 4:43, Yeshua was sent for the purpose of preaching the message of the Kingdom of God. In the first chapter, Luke links Yeshua to the promised king of Israel who will sit on the throne of David. Here the angel reveals it to Miriam (Mary):

> "And behold, you will conceive in your womb and bring forth a Son, and shall call His name Jesus (Yeshua). He will be great, and will be called the Son of the Highest; and the Lord God will give Him the *throne of His father David*. And He will reign over the house of Jacob forever, and of *His kingdom there will be no end.*" (Luke 1:31-33 NKJ)

Hundreds of years before, the prophet Daniel had a vision of this coming King:

> "I was watching in the night visions, And behold, One like the Son of Man, Coming with the clouds of heaven! He came to the Ancient of Days, And they brought Him near before Him. Then to Him was given dominion and glory and a kingdom, That all peoples, nations, and languages should serve Him. His dominion is an everlasting dominion, Which shall not pass away, And His kingdom the one Which shall not be destroyed." (Daniel 7:13-14 NKJ)

The question I would like to raise is this: If we think that we will spend eternity in heaven, why are we asked to pray "your kingdom come to earth as it is in heaven"? What do we have to do with the kingdom on Earth? It appears that the earth will be there in the world to come. This is what Isaiah says when he has a glimpse into it:

> "For behold, I create new heavens and a new earth; and the former shall not be remembered or come to mind." (Isaiah 65:17 NKJ)

John writes:

> "Now I saw a new heaven and a new earth, for the first heaven and the first earth had passed away. Also, there was no more sea." (Revelation 21:1 NKJ)

If we spend eternity in heaven, then what is the purpose of the resurrection from the dead? The resurrection brings us back into the physical world. The focus here is on the world to come (*Ha-Olam Haba*) and not on eternity in heaven. Yeshua uses the term: "The age to come" (Matthew 12:32, Mark 10:30, Luke 18:30). I believe that this wonderful material world will continue in the world to come. But it will be fully saturated with God's presence when heaven and Earth will merge:

> For the earth will be filled with the knowledge of the glory of the Lord, as the waters cover the sea. (Habakkuk 2:14 NKJ)

Following Yeshua's resurrection, He spent the next 40 days with his disciples. During this time, He spoke of only one subject:

> ... to whom He (Yeshua) also presented Himself alive after His suffering by many infallible proofs,

> being seen by them during forty days and speaking of the things pertaining to the kingdom of God. (Acts 1:3 NKJ)

Yeshua started His mission with the message of the kingdom, and He continues with the same message after the resurrection. The book of Acts shows how His disciples echoed this key message.

> But when they believed Philip as he preached the things concerning the kingdom of God and the name of Jesus Christ, both men and women were baptized. (Act 8:12 NKJ)

> And he (Paul) went into the synagogue and spoke boldly for three months, reasoning and persuading concerning the things of the kingdom of God. (Act 19:8 NKJ)

The very last verses of the book of Acts state the following:

> Then Paul dwelt two whole years in his own rented house, and received all who came to him, preaching the kingdom of God and teaching the things which concern the Lord Jesus Christ (Yeshua HaMashiach) with all confidence, no one forbidding him. (Acts 28:30-31 NKJ)

If the message of the kingdom of God is the central message of the Bible, and it is, the question is: How many of us really understand what Yeshua means by the kingdom? Today many people live in democratic societies and do not really understand the concept of a kingdom. A kingdom is not a democracy. In a kingdom, there is no voting. In the true kingdom, the word of the King is law. But what are the essential parts of a kingdom?

1. A kingdom has a king who rules.
2. A kingdom needs people who are ruled by the king.
3. A kingdom has a land on which the king and the people live.
4. A kingdom has laws.

There are some Western countries that have kings or queens. One example is Great Britain. There the king reigns but does not rule. The king has been crowned, sits on a throne, but has no power. The laws are made by the parliament. So, it is not really a true kingdom. The citizens receive all of the benefits of living in a kingdom, but they provide no input. On the other hand, the real and true kingdom is where the king rules and there is no parliament. There the word of the king is law and the king has to be served.

I believe that we are created to live in a kingdom where God is the king. We do not function the way we are supposed to while we live either in a democracy or under the tyranny or dictatorship of men. People often use a democratic system to establish a dictatorship (one example would be Hitler). But our lives will only come to fullness when God is on the throne. In the book of Revelation, we read the following:

> And he showed me a pure river of water of life, clear as crystal, proceeding from the throne of God and of the Lamb. (Rev 22:1 NKJ)

See, true life only comes when God is on the throne. I want to point out that God is sovereign over the entire world; He is in charge – but He is not yet the king of every human being, only the ones who have made Him king over their lives. The king needs people who want him to be king.

But one day God will be the king of everyone.

> The LORD shall reign forever and ever. (Exodus 15:18 NKJ)

> The LORD has established His throne in heaven, and His kingdom rules over all. (Psalm 103:19 NKJ)

> They shall speak of the glory of Your kingdom, and talk of Your power, to make known to the sons of men His mighty acts, and the glorious majesty of His kingdom. Your kingdom is an everlasting kingdom, and Your dominion endures throughout all generations. (Psalm 145:11-13 NKJ)

> And the LORD shall be King over all the earth; in that day shall the LORD be One, and His name one. (Zechariah 14:9 JPS)

Interestingly, the Jewish people in their services sing the song "Avinu Malkeinu" – "Our Father, our king." And it is true; we need to know God as Father and also as the King. The Father loves us and disciplines us; on the other hand, the King must be served.

Let's return to Acts chapter 1. After Yeshua spoke to the disciples for 40 days about the things of the kingdom, the disciples ask Him this question:

THE KINGDOM ON EARTH

Therefore, when they had come together, they asked Him, saying, "Lord, will You at this time *restore* the kingdom to Israel?" (Acts 1:6 NKJ)

Even after hearing the message on the kingdom for 40 days, the disciples are asking when the Kingdom of Israel will be restored. What does restore mean? To me "restore" means that something existed in the past, but it got broken down and it must be fixed to return to what it was. The Greek word here is: ἀποκαθιστάνεις -- *apokathistaneis*, which means restore to the original state or return.

In Acts chapter 3 Peter says:

"Repent therefore and be converted, that your sins may be blotted out, so that times of refreshing may come from the presence of the Lord, and that He may send Yeshua HaMashiach (Jesus Christ), who was preached to you before, whom heaven must receive until the times of restoration of all things, which God has spoken by the mouth of all His holy prophets since the world began." (Acts 3:19-21 NKJ)

Here Peter again talks about the restoration of all things – the same Greek word as in Acts 1:6 – something that existed in the past and is coming back. What things are being restored? We do not have to guess because the text tells us: they are all the things that God spoke by his prophets from ancient times. But why is it that so many people do not know what God is restoring today? The prophets of old spoke, but not everyone knows the prophets well enough.

Martin Luther is the father of the Reformation, but he did not go far enough. He is the father of reformation, but Scripture talks about restoration or return. Luther focused on personal salvation. And this has become the main theme of Christianity. But we will see in this book that personal salvation is only a part of the message of the kingdom of God. There is also national salvation and the salvation of the world.

Does that mean that the kingdom already existed in the past? Apparently, yes. The question: "When will you restore (or return) the kingdom?" indicates this. From biblical history it appears that the kingdom of God has existed at least twice on the earth.

The first kingdom of God on earth was the garden of Eden. There, people were put in charge of the garden. There was only one thing that did not belong to them. That was the tree of the knowledge of good and evil. That tree belonged to God alone and reminded Adam and Eve about the one who was above them, who had authority to determine what is good and what is evil.

The second time the kingdom of God was established was after God took Israel out of Egypt. In this process God judged Egypt with ten plagues. The last plague was the death of the first-born child, and for Israel to avoid it they had to do something. They had to kill the lamb and put its blood on two sides of the door and above it. The blood had to drip to the bottom. So, when the next day the children of Israel came out of their houses to go out of Egypt, they came out through the bloody door, the same way a baby goes through the birth canal of the mother.

At this moment the nation was born. From Egypt they made a journey to Mount Sinai. And there they became a Kingdom, the only kingdom on the planet Earth that had God as the king. This is what God told Moses to tell the children of Israel:

> Now if you obey Me fully and keep My covenant, then out of all nations you will be My treasured possession. Although the whole earth is mine, you will be for me a kingdom of priests and a holy nation. (Exodus 19:5-6 NKJ)

There Israel accepted the proposal:

> The people all responded together, "We will do everything the Lord **has said.**" So Moses brought their answer back to the Lord. (Exodus 19:8 NKJ)

From that point on Israel became the only nation on earth whose King was God. There has not been another kingdom like that. Of course, the kingdom of Israel began to fully function when they entered the land promised to them by God.

For many years Israel did not have a human king. We read in the book of Judges that they were ruled by judges not by kings because God was the king over this nation.

The following verses support this intended form of rulership:

> Then the men of Israel said to Gideon, "Rule over us, both you and your son, and your grandson also; for you have delivered us from the hand of Midian." But Gideon said to them, "I will not rule over you, nor shall my son rule over you; the LORD shall rule over you." (Judges 8:22-23 NKJ)

And when you saw that Nahash king of the Ammonites came against you, you said to me, "No, but a king shall reign over us, *when the LORD your God was your king*." (1Samuel 12:12 NKJ)

Nevertheless, Israel continued to be the kingdom of God on Earth. And God made a promise to King David that his throne would become an eternal throne:

"When your days are fulfilled and you rest with your fathers, I will set up your seed after you, who will come from your body, and I will establish his kingdom. He shall build a house for My name, and I will establish the throne of his kingdom forever." (2 Samuel 7:12-13 NKJ)

The kingdom will be restored to Israel again, but the next time God will reign not just over Israel, but over the entire world. And that will happen when the Messiah will return to Jerusalem and will sit on the throne of David.

"Your seed I will establish forever, and build up your throne to all generations." And the heavens will praise Your wonders, O LORD; Your faithfulness also in the assembly of the saints. (Psalm 89:4-5 NKJ)

I believe that one of the reasons that there is such warfare in the Middle East today is because the kingdom of darkness is at war with the kingdom of God. But the throne of David will be established in Jerusalem, and King Yeshua will sit on it. Yes, the king of the Jews will reign over the entire world.

Remember when Yeshua was on the cross? There was a sign hanging above him that read "Yeshua of Nazareth, King of the Jews." Also, when God sent Moses to talk to the Pharaoh of Egypt, He told Moses to present God as the God of Hebrews.

> ...you and the elders of Israel, to the king of Egypt; and you shall say to him, The LORD God of the Hebrews has met with us ... (Exodus 3:18 NKJ)

The Creator of the universe calls himself the God of the Hebrews. One day the entire world will have to realize that God, the creator of the universe, is the God of the Hebrews.

It's important to understand the deeper meaning of the name Israel. Jacob received the name when he struggled with the Angel of God:

> וַיֹּאמֶר אֵלָיו מַה־שְּׁמֶךָ וַיֹּאמֶר יַעֲקֹב: וַיֹּאמֶר לֹא יַעֲקֹב יֵאָמֵר עוֹד שִׁמְךָ כִּי אִם־יִשְׂרָאֵל כִּי־שָׂרִיתָ עִם־אֱלֹהִים וְעִם־אֲנָשִׁים וַתּוּכָל:
>
> (Gen 32:28-29 WTT)

> So, He said to him, "What is your name?" He said, "Jacob." And He said, "Your name shall no longer be called Jacob, but Israel; for you have struggled with God and with men, and have prevailed." (Gen 32:27-28 NKJ)[2]

Let's look at the word "struggle." In Hebrew the word שָׂרִיתָ (sarita) does not only mean "struggle" but also "to persevere" or "to not give up." The Hebrew translation of the word "prevailed"

---

[2] Verses 27-28 in the English Bible match verses 28-29 in the Hebrew Scriptures.

actually means "being able to." It is possible to translate the last part of the sentence: "... for you have persevered with God and with men, and have been able to." Because Jacob has persevered with God and did not give up, therefore he has gained authority.

The two letters of the root from the word שָׂרִיתָ make a noun שַׂר (sar), which means "a prince or a ruler." If we look at the word "Israel" (יִשְׂרָאֵל) we can see the word שַׂר in it. Now if you put together שַׂר and אֵל – like this: שראל (*sarel*) it means "the ruler of God." The word "Israel" also has the Hebrew letter Yod (י) at the beginning. One of several ways of seeing this is that the Yod turns the word back into a verb in the future tense. So, the first part of the word can mean "will rule" and the second part "God." Thus, both parts that form the word "Israel" mean: "God will rule."[3] I believe that as long as Israel exists, there is a message to all the rulers of the world: You may rule for a while, but one day God will rule. And this is why such warfare exists over the nation and land of Israel.

This verse is read at Christmas all over the world, where the angel tells Miriam about the birth of her son:

> Then the angel said to her, "Do not be afraid, Mary (Miriam), for you have found favor with God. And behold, you will conceive in your womb and bring forth a Son, and **shall call His name Jesus. He will be** great, and will be called the Son of the Highest; and the Lord God will give Him the throne of His father David. *And He will reign over the house of*

---

3 Other messages can be found in the word ישראל, but for the sake of this book we will stay with "God will rule."

THE KINGDOM ON EARTH

Jacob forever, and of His kingdom there will be no end."
(Luke 30-33 NKJ)

Clearly this verse tells us that Miriam's son will become the eternal king of the house of Jacob. What is the house of Jacob? Israel. Yeshua will be king of the whole earth, but first and foremost he is the king of Israel.

I would like to quote one more verse about the kingdom:

> And this gospel of the kingdom will be preached in all the world as a witness to all the nations, and then the end will come. (Mat 24:14 NKJ)

When people get saved all over the world through faith in the atoning death and resurrection of Yeshua, they become part of God's kingdom. They will have to deal with the fact that Israel is the foundation of God's kingdom on Earth. The Heavenly King will come back to Israel and will reign from there over all the earth. Many of the Jewish people have already returned to the Land as the prophets of old have predicted, and many more will come back.

In the next chapter we will look at the four areas relating to the restoration of the Kingdom of God.

2
Four Messages of the Gospel of the Kingdom According to Isaiah

I have mentioned already that the gospel of salvation is only a part of the gospel of the kingdom. The gospel of the kingdom is a much larger subject.

What does the word "gospel" really mean? The English word "gospel" comes from the old English word "godspel," which literally means "God speaks," and in the Bible it is understood as "good news." But in the Hebrew Bible the word that is used is בְּשׂוֹרָה *(besora)* which simply means "news" or "a message." And the person who delivers the news is called מְבַשֵּׂר *(mevaser)*. The biblical use of this term refers to someone who, following a battle or war, delivers a message of victory or defeat.

The prophet Isaiah provides four key insights into this kingdom message.

How beautiful upon the mountains are the feet of him **who brings good news**, who proclaims **peace**, who brings glad tidings of good *things*, who proclaims **salvation**, who says to Zion, "**Your God reigns!**" (Isa 52:7 NKJ)	מַה־נָּאווּ עַל־הֶהָרִים רַגְלֵי מְבַשֵּׂר מַשְׁמִיעַ שָׁלוֹם מְבַשֵּׂר טוֹב מַשְׁמִיעַ יְשׁוּעָה אֹמֵר לְצִיּוֹן מָלַךְ אֱלֹהָיִךְ׃

In this passage, *Mevaser* is translated with five English words: "him who brings good news." This clearly refers to the Messiah.

First He proclaims "peace," or "shalom" (שָׁלוֹם) in Hebrew. The Hebrew noun *shalom* comes from the verb *shilem* or *hishleem* (שָׁלַם or הִשְׁלִים), which means "to complete" or "to pay." Imagine being in a supermarket picking up some milk. But the transaction is not completed until you pay. You pay – אתה משלם – and now you can take the milk. Thus the first kingdom concept God establishes concerns "completion."

Second, in the NKJ version, the *mevaser* brings "glad tidings of good *things*." But the Hebrew text simply says "tov" (טוֹב), which means "good." That is quite a difference! We will delve deeper into this concept of goodness in the next chapter.

Then the messenger announces *yeshuah* (יְשׁוּעָה), which means "salvation." Of course, salvation is a major theme of the kingdom message. In the third chapter of John, Yeshua says that one must be born from above in order to see or enter the kingdom. The message of salvation is a topic rich with layers. We will delve deeper into this concept in chapter 11.

Finally, the passage reads, "say to Zion: Your God reigns" (אָמַר לְצִיּוֹן מָלַךְ אֱלֹהָיִךְ). The word "Zion" has several levels of meaning. In Isaiah this word refers to the nation of Israel, and to be more precise – Jerusalem.

For many centuries Christians traveled to different parts of the world sharing the message of salvation. Multitudes came to salvation in Africa, China, and other countries; but when Christians came to Israel with the same message, it was barely received. What differentiates Israel from other nations? One difference is that Jews feel that if they embrace Christianity, they will cease being Jewish. There is a popular Christian song written on Isaiah 52:7. The refrain of this song goes like this: "Our God reigns." But that is not what Isaiah says. The prophet clearly says, "*Your* God reigns." Jews are not interested in a foreign God who is disconnected from their roots. They do not want to become Christians and stop being Jewish. By contrast, the Bible introduces us to an amazing gentile woman from Moab named Ruth. And this is what she said to her mother-in-law: "Your people are my people, your God is my God" (Ruth 1:16). "Not my God, but your God!"

Christianity's disconnection from its roots has drastically destroyed the ability to fulfill this forth area of the message of the kingdom. What does it really mean to say to them "Your God reigns"? Of course, we live in a time when more and more Christians honor Israel and their Hebraic roots, but Ruth went much further. She identified herself with the people of Israel and with the God of Israel. She did not have a separate religious system anymore; her life was used to heal the heart of her mother-in-law, Naomi, and also to pave the way for the throne of David to become a reality in Israel.

The throne of David is coming back to Israel. And God has a modern-day Ruth to heal the hearts of the people of Israel who have been severely wounded from wars, persecution, Holocaust, terrorist acts, and the list goes on. It is hard to find a family in Israel that has not experienced death or devastation in some way. Israel does not need another religious system. Israel is waiting for Ruth because the same way the throne of God was established in the first place, it will be re-established.

A later chapter is dedicated to a fuller exploration of the book of Ruth. Next, however, we will delve deeper into each of these four areas relating to the establishment of the kingdom of God.

3
Good and Evil

In the previous chapter we talked about four messages of the kingdom as they are mentioned in Isaiah 52:7. In this chapter, I want to focus on the message that is called good. The announcer heralds "good," not "good news" as most translations tell us.

So, what do we understand about this "good"? One of the main questions that needs to be asked is: when did this word appear for the first time in the Bible? The answer is in Genesis 1:4. After God separated light from darkness, the verse says: "God saw that the light was good." In verse 10, we read again: "And God saw that it was good." We find the same phrase in verse 12. Every day of creation ends with the same phrase except day two. The last time this phrase is in verse 31 where we read: "God saw that everything that He had made … was very good" (Gen 1:31). The word good appears seven times in this chapter.

But why does the text say: "God saw…?" Does it mean that God closed His eyes while creating and then He opened them and He liked what he saw? I think what the text is telling us when it says: "God saw" is that He determined what is good. And thus, He defines that what He sees as good is what is right. In Genesis 2, God also tells us what is not good. "…It is not good that man should be alone" (Genesis 2:18 NKJ).

God also determines what is evil:

> "Then the LORD saw that the wickedness of man was great in the earth, and that every intent of the thoughts of his heart was only evil continually." (Genesis 6:5 NKJ).

In this passage, the Hebrew word רע (*Rah*), which means "evil," appears two times. The first time the translator used the word wickedness. He should have translated it like this: "Then the LORD saw that the evil of man was great…"

In chapter one, we mentioned that the kingdom of God on the earth already existed in the past. But when? I believe that the kingdom existed on the earth at least twice according to the biblical descriptions. The Garden of Eden was the first kingdom of God on Earth. After God created people and planted the garden in Eden, he put them in the garden and put them in charge over everything. Everything belonged to them except for one thing: the tree. The tree of the knowledge of good and evil did not belong to people, but to God. As long as the tree was there, it reminded Adam and Eve that even though they had the charge of the garden of Eden, there was someone above them – the Heavenly King.

> The Lord God planted a garden eastward in Eden, and there He put the man whom He had formed. And out of the ground the Lord God made every tree grow that is pleasant to the sight and good for food. The tree of life *was* also in the midst of the garden, and the tree of the knowledge of good and evil. Genesis 2:8-9

Where was the tree of life? *In the midst* of the garden (inside, not necessarily in the middle). Where was the tree of the knowledge of good and evil? The text does not say (check the verse again). Why? Of course, the context suggests that the tree of the knowledge of good and evil was also in the midst of the garden. But why would the text not state it explicitly: "The tree of life and the tree of the knowledge of good and evil were in the midst of the garden." Why does the text present it like this? "The tree of life *was* also in the midst of the garden, *and the tree of the knowledge of good and evil.*" I think the text is focusing on what God most wants to impart to us – which is the tree of life. And that is what the text is highlighting. The Garden of Eden was the place of choice for Adam and Eve. There God was commanding what to choose – life or death, just like the choice that God presented before the Israelites as they were about to take possession of the land:

> "I call heaven and earth as witnesses today against you, that I have set before you life and death, blessing and cursing; therefore choose life, that both you and your descendants may live." (Deuteronomy 30:19 NKJ)

God tells Israel what to choose: "choose life." The same way God commanded Adam to choose.

All of this raises another question: How many commandments were given in the garden? Most people see only one commandment. But let's take a look.

> And the Lord God commanded the man, saying, "Of every tree of the garden you may freely eat." (Genesis 2:16 NKJ)

This looks to me like a command. And then it says:

> "... but of the tree of the knowledge of good and evil you shall not eat, for in the day that you eat of it you shall surely die." (Genesis 2:17 NKJ)

That looks like another command. There are two commandments, not one.

The English translation in verse 16 is not very accurate here: "Of every tree of the garden you may freely eat." But in the Hebrew text there is a double verb used here (אָכֹל תֹּאכֵל), which actually is a strong command. It should say, "not may freely, but must eat." But in verse 17 the translator renders the double verb correctly: (מוֹת תָּמוּת) – "you will surely die."

Notice what happens in chapter three. Here the snake and the woman are having a conversation:

> And the woman said to the serpent, "We may eat the fruit of the trees of the garden; but of the fruit of the tree which *is* in the midst of the garden, God has said, 'You shall not eat it, nor shall you touch it, lest you die.'" (Genesis 3:2-3 NKJ)

Let's compare this with the text in Genesis 2:

Text in Genesis 2:9b	From Genesis 3:3
The tree of life was also in the midst of the garden, and the tree of the knowledge of good and evil.	...*but of the fruit of the tree* which *is* in the midst of the garden, God has said, 'You shall not eat it, nor shall you touch it, lest you die.'

The woman is speaking of the tree of the knowledge of good and evil in the midst of the garden. On the other hand, the text in Genesis 2:9 says that the tree of life was in the midst of the garden. I have already mentioned that according to the context both trees are in the midst of the garden. But the text in Genesis 2:9 is focusing on the tree of life which God desires for mankind, while in chapter 3 the woman is focusing on the tree which she desires. The text is showing that the woman and the man – who was with her and heard the entire dialogue that she had with the snake – strongly desired the fruit from the forbidden tree. And the snake encouraged the woman to give in to her desire.

Clearly, both human beings and animals have strong desires. But the difference is that the animals live by instincts, whereas people are called to live by the word of God and not just to obey every desire that they have. God wanted us to learn to rule over our desires. Of course, there is nothing wrong with having the desires. God made us with desires that come from our hearts. Life would be very boring without desires. But we must submit to God's word above our desires or else we will become slaves to the evil desires that our hearts will produce.

And why did they desire fruit from this tree when there were so many other trees to eat from? I believe they wanted the hidden knowledge that they believed the tree had, the knowledge of good and evil. This knowledge only belongs to God. Eating from the tree of the knowledge of good and evil would make them like God, knowing everything. Then they would not need God at all; they would become absolute rulers.

Let's see what happens in verse 6:

> "So when the woman saw that the tree *was* good for food, that it *was* pleasant to the eyes, and a tree *desirable* to make *one wise*, she took of its fruit and ate." (Genesis 3:6 NKJ)

The woman saw that the tree was good… Who is now making determination regarding what is good? A woman. She desires the knowledge that does not belong to her, that only belongs to the Heavenly King. By determining what is good, she usurps the King's authority. And what about the man? He was standing next to her listening to the whole conversation between the woman and the snake and did nothing to stop this. ("She also gave to her husband *with her*, and he ate.") He is the one who received the commandment, and when the spirit of darkness reached out to his wife, he did nothing.

Both of them moved into a realm that did not belong to them. They usurped the authority of their King and became like God themselves, knowing good and evil. God himself confirms this in Genesis 3:22a.

> Then the Lord God said, "Behold, the man has become like one of Us, to know good and evil…"

Now man determines what is good and what is evil. How does God decide what is good and what is evil? According to His desire. Similarly, people also determine what is good and what is evil according to their own desires. And since they gave into their desires in the garden, its power has increased and rules their hearts.

This is how we use the words good and evil today. I will say, "I like chocolate; it is good!" "But celery I do not like; it is bad!"

GOOD AND EVIL

The word for "evil" in Hebrew is "rah" (רַע). It also means "bad." Clearly, we use the words good and bad in a very subjective way. Likewise, we use the same words for our moral standards, and that can be extremely dangerous. For instance, Hitler wanted to eradicate all Jews, Gypsies, and others, thinking this would make the world a better place. According to him, killing innocent people was good. And he was not alone in this opinion. This world has been corrupted by people determining for themselves what is good and what is evil. We desperately need the return of God's kingdom, where God rules and teaches us what is good and what is evil, what is right and what is wrong. Of course, today we have His Word that teaches us exactly this, and we have the Holy Spirit to give us power to rule over our own desires. There is nothing wrong with desires when they are operating within the framework of the Word of God. But when the desires get out of control, they become destructive.

Psalm 16:2 says it all:

> I say to the LORD, "You are my Lord; I have no good apart from you." (ESV)

The psalmist understands that good comes only from God. Yeshua once had a conversation with a rich young ruler:

> Now as He was going out on the road, one came running, knelt before Him, and asked Him, "Good Teacher, what shall I do that I may inherit eternal life?" So Jesus said to him, "Why do you call Me good? No one *is* good but One, *that is,* God." (Mark 10: 17-18)

Yeshua Himself establishes the fact that only God is good. It is His goodness that needs to be in us and in this world.

4
Lech Lecha

Let's take a deeper look at what took place after the first man and woman disobeyed God. Scripture tells us that their eyes were opened and they saw they were naked. So they covered themselves with fig leaves. Suddenly they heard the voice of the Lord God walking in the garden, and they hid themselves. In verse 9, God asks Adam a question: "Where are you?" This is strange! Doesn't all-knowing God know where Adam is?

The Hebrew word that is used here is: אַיֶּכָּה – pronounced: Ah-ye-ka. The first part אַי (ah-ye) means *where* and the second part means *you*. Ah-ye does not necessarily deal with location. God is simply telling Adam: "You are not here; you are gone." The deeper meaning: "You are lost; you are no longer with Me; you do not even know who you really are anymore." Adam then tells God:

> "I heard Your voice in the garden, and I was afraid because I was naked; and I hid myself." (Genesis 3:10)

Adam was afraid not only because he heard God's voice, but also because he saw his own nakedness. He was naked before, but that did not bother him because his focus was God. But now he looks at himself. And he is afraid. He has lost his identity, and he does not know who he is anymore because he has stepped into an area that belongs to the King. From this point, humans' actions are based on fear – the fear of being lost.

People were created in the image of God. And one of the major gifts they received from God is creativity. God is a great creator. People are little creators. But now people rely on their creativity to find identity. In Genesis 11, people use their creativity to build a city and a tower in the land of Shinar in order to make names for themselves. They are driven by the fear of being scattered and lost. But they got lost and scattered anyway. They built a city named Babel, which means confusion. God confused their languages, leading to their being confused about their identities.

Following the story of Babel, we are first introduced to Abraham. Here are the famous words that God spoke to Abraham:

| Now the Lord had said to Abram: "Get out of your country, from your family and from your father's house, to a land that I will show you. I will make you a great nation; I will bless you, and make your name great; and you shall be a blessing. I will bless those who bless you, and I will curse him who curses you; and in you all the families of the earth shall be blessed." (Genesis 12:1-3 NKJ) | וַיֹּאמֶר יְהוָה אֶל־אַבְרָם, לֶךְ־לְךָ מֵאַרְצְךָ וּמִמּוֹלַדְתְּךָ וּמִבֵּית אָבִיךָ, אֶל־הָאָרֶץ, אֲשֶׁר אַרְאֶךָּ. וְאֶעֶשְׂךָ לְגוֹי גָּדוֹל וַאֲבָרֶכְךָ וַאֲגַדְּלָה שְׁמֶךָ וֶהְיֵה בְּרָכָה. וַאֲבָרֲכָה מְבָרְכֶיךָ וּמְקַלֶּלְךָ אָאֹר וְנִבְרְכוּ בְךָ כֹּל מִשְׁפְּחֹת הָאֲדָמָה. |

LECH LECHA

God asks Abraham to leave his hometown. He is not telling him exactly where, just "to a land that I will show you." Strange! Having no final destination, Abraham is totally dependent on God to show him where to go. But so far all of the narrative details relate to what Abraham is leaving behind: his land, his birthplace, and his father's house. Why? Isn't it enough to say: "Go from this place to that place?" I believe that the text wants to take us deeper and to show a spiritual transformation of the inner man.

Abraham was born in Babylonia; he grew up in the kingdom of Nimrod, the kingdom of confusion. What kind of identity was formed in him as he was growing up? What kind of values did he receive from his Babylonian culture, from his father's house? What kind of words did he hear from his parents as a child and young man?

Let's take a closer look at the passage we just read. The New King James version renders the command as "get out." But the Hebrew reads differently. It says: לך-לך (*lech lecha*). *Lech* is the imperative form of the word "go" or "walk." But *lecha* means "to you" or "to yourself." Go to yourself? Interesting! Isn't it enough just to say go? Why to yourself?

Growing up in the kingdom of Nimrod, Abraham does know his true identity. And now what God is saying to him: "If you follow Me, I will take you to yourself; you will find yourself and know who you really are."

What we can glean from this story is that none of us will truly know who we are by focusing on ourselves. But if we know who He is then we will know who we are. This message is for all of us. By following Him, looking to Him, we will leave our sinful past, even the sins of our fathers and of previous generations. And we will come to our true identity because it only can come from our Father in Heaven. Only in Him will we know our true value.

These verses from the Psalms echo this message:

> Listen, O daughter, consider and incline your ear; forget your own people also, and your father's house; so the King will greatly desire your beauty; because He *is* **your Lord, worship Him. (Psalm 45:10-11 NKJ)**

When the text tells us this, "listen, consider, incline your ear…," these are three different ways to say "pay attention." What comes next is very important: "Forget your people and your father's house…" This is what God also told Abraham. It doesn't mean we shouldn't call our father ever again. It simply means that if we look to God and worship Him alone, He will show us how beautiful we are to Him and how much He desires us.

Abraham's journey was designed to shift his focus from his father's house to his Heavenly Father's. God's desire has always been to reveal Himself to the lost.

Father is the source of love. Yeshua walked in the love of His Father. And He was able to demonstrate His Father to the world. He once said: "I am the way, the truth, and the life. No one comes to the Father except through Me" (John 14:6 NKJ).

So perhaps we can better understand why Isaiah tells us: "Look to Abraham your father, and to Sarah *who* **bore you…" (Isaiah 51:2 NKJ)**.

There are eternal things we can learn from the lives of our forefathers and foremothers with whom God made eternal covenant. Abraham and Sarah are the foundation on which God began to build His kingdom.

5
Nimrod

In this chapter, I'd like to look at the first kingdom built by man. The king of this kingdom is mentioned very little in the Bible. Yet he had one of the most profound influences on all of humanity. His name was Nimrod.

We meet him for the first time in Genesis chapter 10. This chapter has genealogies of the three sons of Noah: Ham, Shem, and Japheth. Here we gain insight into the beginning of the different nations that developed after the flood.

Four generations from Noah, Nimrod is born. The verses about Nimrod include a small description.

Cush begot Nimrod; he began to be a mighty one on the earth. He was a mighty hunter before the Lord; therefore it is said, "Like Nimrod the mighty hunter before the Lord." And the beginning of his kingdom was Babel, Erech, Accad, and Calneh, in the land of Shinar. (Genesis 10:8-10)	כּוּשׁ, יָלַד אֶת-נִמְרֹד; הוּא הֵחֵל, לִהְיוֹת גִּבֹּר בָּאָרֶץ. הוּא-הָיָה גִבֹּר-צַיִד, לִפְנֵי יְהוָה; עַל-כֵּן, יֵאָמַר, כְּנִמְרֹד גִּבּוֹר צַיִד, לִפְנֵי יְהוָה. וַתְּהִי רֵאשִׁית מַמְלַכְתּוֹ בָּבֶל, וְאֶרֶךְ וְאַכַּד וְכַלְנֵה, בְּאֶרֶץ שִׁנְעָר.

Genesis 10:8 says that he was a "mighty one in the earth." And in verse 9 we read: "he was a mighty hunter before the Lord."

The question is: What does it mean that he was "mighty on earth"? The Hebrew word גִּבֹּר (*gibor*) suggests that he was a very powerful man. When it says גִּבֹּר בָּאָרֶץ (*gibor baarez*) it could even mean that he was the most powerful man on earth. What then does "mighty hunter before the Lord" have to do with him being "mighty on earth"? It seems like there is not much connection between these two statements. To get a deeper insight, let's read verse 10 again.

> And the beginning of his kingdom was Babel, Erech, Accad, and Calneh, in the land of Shinar. (Genesis 10:10 NKJ)

וַתְּהִי רֵאשִׁית מַמְלַכְתּוֹ בָּבֶל וְאֶרֶךְ וְאַכַּד וְכַלְנֵה בְּאֶרֶץ שִׁנְעָר:

This verse gives us more insight into Nimrod. He actually was a king who built his kingdom beginning with Babel (pronounced in Hebrew בָּבֶל (*bavel*). *Bavel* means "confusion." The name is fitting, as God later confused the languages of those who arrogantly built the tower (Genesis 11:7). So Nimrod's kingdom was the kingdom of confusion, also full of ungodliness and idolatry. But why is Nimrod called a "mighty hunter before the Lord." Is this a positive or negative statement? How can it be positive since Nimrod built a pagan kingdom?

The name Nimrod in Hebrew looks like this: נִמְרוֹד. Inside the name we see the word: מֶרֶד (*mered*), which means "rebel." Thus the word *nimrod* actually means "we will rebel" or "let us rebel." You may ask what kind of father and mother would call their

NIMROD

child "we will rebel"? They probably gave him a different name, but Nimrod is the name that the biblical text uses to give us an insight into his character and who he really was.

But why was this rebellious king called "the mighty hunter before the Lord"? Let me explain the Hebrew word לִפְנֵי (*lifney*), which means before. It simply represents a position. The word *lifney* is based on the word that means "face." Imagine two armies stand facing each other, and they are about to engage in a battle. Thus, depending on the situation, this word can mean "before" or "against." Nimrod was a mighty hunter in the face of God. The question is: Was he really hunting animals? Or was it something else? In ancient times, great leaders often were described in the act of hunting. Note what the well-known historian Josephus wrote about Nimrod:

> Now it was Nimrod who excited them to such an affront and contempt of God. He was the grand-son of Ham, the son of Noah: a bold man, and of great strength of hand. He persuaded them not to ascribe it to God, as if it was through his means that they were happy; but to believe that it was their own courage which procured that happiness. He also gradually changed the government into tyranny; seeing no other way of turning men from the fear of God, but to bring them into a constant dependence on his own power. He also said, "He would be revenged on God, if he should have a mind to drown the world again: for that he would build a Tower too high for the waters to be able to reach; and that he would avenge

himself on God for destroying their fore-fathers."
(Flavius Josephus of the Antiquities of the Jews — Book I, chapter 4)

It appears that Nimrod was the first dictator. And he tried to subdue all of humankind. He wasn't hunting for animals; he was hunting for people. He is, actually, found in much of the pagan literature. One of his names is Gilgamesh. He was the father of paganism, and he became god in many pagan religions. For example, in Greek mythology he is called Zeus, in the Roman world, Jupiter.[1]

I believe that the spirit of Nimrod is felt today in every sphere of our society – both religious and secular. Every organization, including businesses and religious denominations, can become kingdoms where people rule ruthlessly without fear of God, imposing control over everyone under them. Many people have been injured by religious leaders who have created their own systems, which became their kingdoms. By thinking that we serve God, we actually serve these systems. Such systems suck the life out of us, and if we leave them, they go after us, strike us in the back. And then people cut us off and tell others not to associate with us. We need to learn to understand the difference between control, which is the work of the flesh, and authority, which is the work of the Spirit.

But the kingdom of God does not fit into any of our systems. Sadly, the spirit of ungodly control (vs. true authority in God) is taking over people's lives.

In Genesis chapter 3, we saw how Adam and Eve (and thus humankind) lost their identity in the garden. God asked a very pro-

---

1 The Two Babylons by Alexander Hislop

found question: "Where are you, Adam?" Humans tried to wrest rulership from God, resulting in a loss of their oneness with Him.

In the previous chapter we talked about how humankind demonstrated a loss of identity by building the city and the tower of Babel (Genesis 11). They used their creativity to build their name. The gift of creativity is given to us by God. God made us in His image and His likeness. Because He is the creator, we are also creators. But creativity can be destructive if not properly managed. With our creativity we can destroy when we are not submitted to God's authority. But our true purpose is to be co-creators with God to advance His kingdom. If we do not understand our true identity, then we use our creativity to build a false identity based on works. Not knowing who they were, the tower builders tried to make a name for themselves. When we do not know who we are, we try to focus on ourselves, trying to build ourselves.

There is a man in the Bible who was chosen to be in charge of building God's tabernacle (Exodus 31:1-11). His name is Bezalel. The tabernacle was the place of God's habitation with his people here on Earth. In Hebrew, Bezalel is written like this: בצלאל. It is pronounced be-tzel-el. צֵל (*Tzel*) in Hebrew means shadow. So, his name means: "in the shadow of God." The word *tzel* is close to the word צֶלֶם (*tzelem*), which means image. Bezalel means: in the shadow or in the image of God. And this man who is made in God's image is building a dwelling place for God in our world. This is a picture of creativity appropriately applied, where we work alongside God as co-builders. But in the Kingdom of Nimrod there is no true identity; people have to secure their own legacy. They were afraid to be scattered but got scattered anyway. Their languages got confused because the kingdom of Nimrod is the kingdom of confusion. Today the kingdom of Nimrod has infiltrated every sphere of our lives, and unless we give ourselves to God we end up getting entangled with Nimrod.

So let us take our eyes off ourselves and look to Him – the author and the finisher of our faith, the One who gives our lives true meaning.

6
The Hidden Elephant

When the children of Israel fled Egypt passing through the bloody door like a baby going through the birth canal, they became a nation. Fifty days later they stood at Mount Sinai, in the place called Horeb (Exodus 19). There they became the kingdom. From that point on, Israel was the only nation on earth ever to have God, the creator of the universe, as their king. And what happened at Mount Sinai is reflected in many parts of Scripture. This is how Moses describes it to the next generation of Israelites in Deuteronomy 4:11-13.

> Then you came near and stood at the foot of the mountain, and the mountain burned with fire to the midst of heaven, with darkness, cloud, and thick darkness. And the Lord spoke to you out of the midst of the fire. You heard the sound of the words, but saw no form; *you* only *heard* a voice. So He declared to you His covenant which He commanded you to perform, the Ten Commandments; and He wrote them on two tablets of stone. (Deuteronomy 4:11-13 NKJ)

This is a terrifying picture: darkness, clouds, a shaking mountain. Nobody sees God. The entire nation hears His voice at least for some time, until they cannot take it anymore and ask Moses to talk to God alone (Exodus 20:15).

Notice what Moses says about Israel becoming the kingdom of God in these passages from Exodus 19:

| Now therefore, if you will indeed obey My voice and keep My covenant, then you shall be a special treasure to Me above all people; for all the earth *is* Mine. (Exodus 19:5 NKJ) | וְעַתָּה, אִם-שָׁמוֹעַ תִּשְׁמְעוּ בְּקֹלִי, וּשְׁמַרְתֶּם, אֶת-בְּרִיתִי--וִהְיִיתֶם לִי סְגֻלָּה מִכָּל-הָעַמִּים, כִּי-לִי כָּל-הָאָרֶץ. |

God promises that the people of Israel will be to Him a special treasure. In Hebrew the word is: סְגֻלָּה (*s'gula*), which refers to something so precious that the king keeps it in his treasure chest. *S'gula* relates to the word – סָגֹל (*sagol*) – the color of purple. Purple garments were very expensive clothing. Often kings wore purple garments (Judges 8:26), which became the color of royalty. God promises to make Israel royalty, a dramatic turnaround after having been slaves in Egypt. But the conditions are to obey God's voice and to keep His covenant. The word here is a double verb in Hebrew: שָׁמוֹעַ תִּשְׁמְעוּ (*shamoa tishmeoo*). It comes from the root שמע (*shama*), which means to hear and respond (not just to hear). The double verb means that the command is very strong. This verb שמע is used in the other part of the scripture that is recited today at every service in every synagogue around the world:

| Hear, O Israel: The Lord our God, the Lord *is* one! (Deuteronomy 6:4 NKJ) | שְׁמַע יִשְׂרָאֵל: יְהוָה אֱלֹהֵינוּ, יְהוָה אֶחָד |

Back to Exodus 19:

| And you shall be to Me a kingdom of priests and a holy nation. These *are* the words which you shall speak to the children of Israel. (Exodus 19:6 NKJ) | וְאַתֶּם תִּהְיוּ-לִי מַמְלֶכֶת כֹּהֲנִים, וְגוֹי קָדוֹשׁ: אֵלֶּה, הַדְּבָרִים, אֲשֶׁר תְּדַבֵּר, אֶל-בְּנֵי יִשְׂרָאֵל |

What is the function of the priest besides performing sacrifices?

| For the lips of a priest should keep knowledge, and people should seek the law from his mouth; for he is the messenger of the Lord of hosts. (Malachi 2:7 NKJ) | כִּי-שִׂפְתֵי כֹהֵן יִשְׁמְרוּ-דַעַת, וְתוֹרָה יְבַקְשׁוּ מִפִּיהוּ: כִּי מַלְאַךְ יְהוָה-צְבָאוֹת, הוּא |

The priests were to represent the character and the ways of God to the people. The kingdom nation is to represent the heavenly kingdom on Earth.

Let's look at a few more points in Exodus chapter 19. In verse 8, the children of Israel accept the covenant:

> The people all responded together, "We will do everything the Lord has said." So Moses brought their answer back to the Lord.

Then God commands them to consecrate themselves, wash their clothes, and not approach the mountain until they hear the sound of the shofar. Verse 13b:

Only when the ram's horn sounds a long blast may they approach the mountain. (Exodus 19:13 NKJ)	בִּמְשֹׁךְ, הַיֹּבֵל, הֵמָּה, יַעֲלוּ בָהָר

The Hebrew word that is used for the ram's horn here is *hayovel*. It means jubilee. How do we know it is a shofar? Verse 16 specifies the word, here translated as "trumpet." The Hebrew text says *shofar*.

On the morning of the third day there was thunder and lightning, with a thick cloud over the mountain, and a very loud trumpet blast. Everyone in the camp trembled. (Exodus 19:16 NKJ)	וַיְהִי בַיּוֹם הַשְּׁלִישִׁי בִּהְיֹת הַבֹּקֶר, וַיְהִי קֹלֹת וּבְרָקִים וְעָנָן כָּבֵד עַל-הָהָר, וְקֹל **שֹׁפָר**, חָזָק מְאֹד; וַיֶּחֱרַד כָּל-הָעָם, אֲשֶׁר בַּמַּחֲנֶה

That is the sound of the shofar of Jubilee. Elsewhere, we read about the shofar in Leviticus 25:9-10. It is blown on the Day of Atonement and announces the coming of the year of Jubilee. Two things will take place on the year of Jubilee. If someone is sold into slavery, he goes free. If a landowner was forced to sell his property, it reverts back to his ownership. For Israel this was the time of Jubilee: They are dramatically freed from slavery, and they are about to inherit the land promised to them by God.

Now the sound of the shofar is heard strong and loud. But who was blowing the shofar? It doesn't appear that anyone from Israel's camp was blowing the shofar at this holy moment. I believe that it was the voice of God that sounded like the shofar, as we read earlier in Deuteronomy 4:12:

> "You heard the sound of the words, but saw no form; *you* only *heard* a voice."

First and foremost, the shofar represents God's voice.

| And when the blast of the trumpet sounded long and became louder and louder, Moses spoke, and God answered him by voice. (Exodus 19:19 NKJ) | וַיְהִי קוֹל הַשֹּׁפָר, **הוֹלֵךְ** וְחָזֵק **מְאֹד**; מֹשֶׁה יְדַבֵּר, וְהָאֱלֹהִים יַעֲנֶנּוּ בְקוֹל. |

There is a very interesting detail here. In English it says that the blast of the trumpet sounded long and became louder and louder. But in Hebrew the verse literally says: the sound (or the voice) of the shofar *walks and very strong*. What does it mean: "the voice walks"? Translators seem to find the phrase nonsensical. I do believe the sound of the shofar was increasing. Imagine God Himself is getting closer and closer and His voice is getting louder and stronger. But the reason the text says "walking" is because there is a deeper meaning here. Where else have we seen the "walking voice of God" in the Bible? Of course, in the Garden of Eden. And that happened after the first man and woman disobeyed and ate from the forbidden tree.

| And they heard the *sound (voice) of the Lord God walking in the garden* in the cool of the day, and Adam and his wife hid themselves from the presence of the Lord God among the trees of the garden. (Genesis 3:8 NKJ) | וַיִּשְׁמְעוּ אֶת-קוֹל יְהוָה אֱלֹהִים, מִתְהַלֵּךְ בַּגָּן-לְרוּחַ הַיּוֹם; וַיִּתְחַבֵּא הָאָדָם וְאִשְׁתּוֹ, מִפְּנֵי יְהוָה אֱלֹהִים, בְּתוֹךְ, עֵץ הַגָּן. |

In the garden, Adam and Eve dismissed God from being the King. What would have happened if they responded differently after hearing the walking voice of God? What if they repented instead of defending themselves? Maybe things would have turned out differently. Instead, Adam responded defensively and blamed both God and Eve.

> Then the man said, "The woman whom You gave *to be* with me, she gave me of the tree, and I ate." (Genesis 3:12 NKJ)

So one of the significant things that transpired at Sinai was the reversal of what happened in Eden when Adam and Eve rejected God as their King. At Sinai, God became King over the entire nation of Israel. Here we see a process set in motion that will lead to the redemption of humankind.

Israel enters into the marriage covenant with God. But in the years to come, they are not always faithful to the covenant. Many times they break it and end up in exile.

'For I am with you,' says the Lord, 'to save you; Though I make a full end of all nations where I have scattered you, yet I will not make a complete end of you. But I will correct you in justice, and will not let you go altogether unpunished.' (Jeremiah 30:11 NKJ)	כִּי-אִתְּךָ אֲנִי נְאֻם-יְהוָה, לְהוֹשִׁיעֶךָ: כִּי אֶעֱשֶׂה כָלָה בְּכָל-הַגּוֹיִם אֲשֶׁר הֲפִצוֹתִיךָ שָּׁם, אַךְ אֹתְךָ לֹא-אֶעֱשֶׂה כָלָה, וְיִסַּרְתִּיךָ לַמִּשְׁפָּט, וְנַקֵּה לֹא אֲנַקֶּךָּ.

In the next chapter of Jeremiah, God promises a new or renewed covenant to Israel:

> Behold, the days are coming, says the Lord, when *I will make a new covenant with the house of Israel and with the house of Judah* -- not according to the covenant that I made with their fathers in the day that I took them by the hand to lead them out of the land of Egypt, My covenant which they broke, though I was a husband to them, says the Lord. But this is the covenant that I will make with the house of Israel after those days, says the Lord: I will put My law in their minds, and write it on their hearts; and I will be their God, and they shall be My people. (Jeremiah 31:31-33 NKJ)
>
> הִנֵּה יָמִים בָּאִים נְאֻם־יְהוָה וְכָרַתִּי אֶת־בֵּית יִשְׂרָאֵל וְאֶת־בֵּית יְהוּדָה בְּרִית חֲדָשָׁה: לֹא כַבְּרִית אֲשֶׁר כָּרַתִּי אֶת־אֲבוֹתָם בְּיוֹם הֶחֱזִיקִי בְיָדָם לְהוֹצִיאָם מֵאֶרֶץ מִצְרָיִם אֲשֶׁר־הֵמָּה הֵפֵרוּ אֶת־בְּרִיתִי וְאָנֹכִי בָּעַלְתִּי בָם נְאֻם־יְהוָה: כִּי זֹאת הַבְּרִית אֲשֶׁר אֶכְרֹת אֶת־בֵּית יִשְׂרָאֵל אַחֲרֵי הַיָּמִים הָהֵם נְאֻם־יְהוָה נָתַתִּי אֶת־תּוֹרָתִי בְּקִרְבָּם וְעַל־לִבָּם אֶכְתֲּבֶנָּה וְהָיִיתִי לָהֶם לֵאלֹהִים וְהֵמָּה יִהְיוּ־לִי לְעָם:

Here God is describing his relationship to Israel in the first covenant as their husband. And it is the same relationship in the New Covenant. As we read the texts, this question arises: with whom is God making this New Covenant? The answer is simple, with the house of Israel and the house of Judah. Did God make the new covenant with Americans? Or Russians, Europeans, Africans, Indians, or any other nation? The answer is: "No!" So what about the people from the nations who believe in the God of Abraham through Yeshua? They have received a gift of love from above and are ingrafted into the covenant that God made with Israel, for there is no separate covenant.

Your God, the creator of the universe, is called God of Hebrews (Exodus 7:16). Your savior is the King of the Jews (John 19:19). You have been joined to the kingdom nation called Israel. You do not have to be Jewish to be part of this kingdom. Abraham was not Jewish; Ruth was not Jewish. You did not replace the original descendants of Abraham but joined them together as one new man. You have an amazing inheritance worth exploring. For in this kingdom of God, you have a specific and unique role to fulfill.

It is strange that so many people do not see that Israel is vital in the establishment of the Kingdom of God. Israel is like the hidden elephant that one day will shock everyone by its size and significance.

7
The Children of Eber

In this chapter we will see how God's second kingdom on Earth started at the same time as Nimrod was building his. Let's take a look at the genealogy of Shem:

> And children were born also to Shem, *the father of all the children of Eber,* the brother of Japheth the elder. (Genesis 10:21 NKJ)

It says here that Shem is *the father of all the children of Eber.* Who is Eber and who are his children? Also, why is he mentioned here at the beginning of the genealogy since he is the fourth generation in the line of Shem?

> And *children* were born also to Shem, the father of all the children of Eber, the brother of Japheth the elder. The sons of Shem *were* Elam, Asshur, Arphaxad, Lud, and Aram. The sons of Aram *were* Uz, Hul, Gether, and Mash. Arphaxad begot Salah, and Salah begot Eber. (Genesis 10:22-23 NKJ)

This is how the genealogy of Shem looks:

Shem
Arphaxad
Salah
Eber

Eber's name is pronounced in Hebrew עֵבֶר (*ever*). Let's take a closer look at why he's so important in the biblical genealogy.

To Eber were born two sons: the name of one *was* Peleg, for in his days the earth was divided; and his brother's name *was* Joktan. (Genesis 10:25 NKJ)	וּלְעֵבֶר יֻלַּד, שְׁנֵי בָנִים: שֵׁם הָאֶחָד **פֶּלֶג**, כִּי בְיָמָיו **נִפְלְגָה** הָאָרֶץ, וְשֵׁם אָחִיו, יָקְטָן.

So, Eber had two children: Peleg (פֶּלֶג) and Joktan (יָקְטָן). Peleg receives a small description: "…for in his days the earth was divided." While there's little here to go on, the question is raised: "What does this mean?" As we continue to read, the text provides the names of the descendants of Joktan. What about Peleg? This information about the earth being divided cannot be just trivia. Perhaps the meaning of his name will give us some understanding.

The word פֶּלֶג *(peleg)* as a noun means "a stream." And the verb פלג means "to divide" or "to separate." In the text above, פלג is the name of Eber's son, and נפלגה *(niflega)* means divided. You can see the word פלג inside נפלגה. Here are all the meanings of the word *peleg*: division, fraction, or a stream.

What does it all mean? Peleg lived in the days of Nimrod. In the previous chapter we learned that Nimrod built his kingdom and that he was mighty on the earth. He united people under his

THE CHILDREN OF EBER

leadership. The keyword here is earth. While Nimrod was trying to unite the earth under his rule, in Peleg's days the earth was divided.

Historically, the days of Peleg most likely refers to the building of the tower, the confusion of the languages, and the various people groups then being scattered. Not surprisingly, the text also reveals a spiritual insight. While Nimrod was uniting people under his leadership to build his kingdom, Peleg and his descendants did not submit to this one-world government and instead separated from it.

In Genesis 11, after the tower-building story, starting with verse 10, the genealogy of Shem is repeated again. This time the genealogy focuses on Peleg's descendants, bringing us all the way to Abram (pronounced av-ram in Hebrew). Here even the genealogy of Peleg is separated. More than that, the name of Peleg's father, Eber (עבר), also has a special meaning. As a verb it means "to cross over" or "to go to the other side." So, while Nimrod is building his kingdom in the land of Shinar, God begins to build His on the other side.

Thus the stream (*peleg*) begins to flow in a different direction, opposite to the stream of Nimrod. Then the genealogy of Peleg brings us all the way to Abram. This stream is the beginning of the river of life as it is described in this psalm:

> There is a river whose streams shall make glad the city of God, the holy place of the tabernacle of the Most High. God is in the midst of her, she shall not be moved; God shall help her, just at the break of dawn. (Psalm 46:5-6 NKJ)
>
> נָהָר--פְּלָגָיו, יְשַׂמְּחוּ עִיר-אֱלֹהִים; קְדֹשׁ, מִשְׁכְּנֵי עֶלְיוֹן. אֱלֹהִים בְּקִרְבָּהּ, בַּל-תִּמּוֹט; יַעְזְרֶהָ אֱלֹהִים, לִפְנוֹת בֹּקֶר.

Here the word for streams is פלגיו (*plagav*), which literary means "his streams." God's river of life appears several times in Scripture, including Ezekiel 47 and Revelation 22:1. Usually the rivers are fed by the streams. But God's stream is separate from the river of Nimrod's kingdom. It becomes God's River.

At this point we are introduced to Abram (אברם). God tells Abram to go to the place that He would show him. Abram obeys God and follows Him. In Genesis 14:13, for the first time, Abram is called "Abram the Hebrew" (*Avram haivri* - העברי). "Ha" is the definite article, and "*ivri*" means Hebrew. Compare the word עברי (*ivri*) to the name עבר (Eber) (pronounced e-ver), the great-grandson of Shem. Now we can see why Eber is mentioned at the top of Shem's genealogy:

> And *children* were born also to Shem, the father of all the children of Eber, the brother of Japheth the elder. (Genesis 10:21 NKJ)

The children of Eber are the Hebrew people.

As we saw earlier, the verb עָבַר (*avar*) in Hebrew means "to cross over." So, the Hebrew people are the ones who cross over to the other side on a regular basis. Abraham left Babylonia, the place of confusion, and crossed over to the other side.

Abram passed through the land to the place of Shechem, as far as the terebinth tree of Moreh. And the Canaanites *were* then in the land. (Genesis 12:6)	וַיַּעֲבֹר אַבְרָם, בָּאָרֶץ, עַד מְקוֹם שְׁכֶם, עַד אֵלוֹן מוֹרֶה; וְהַכְּנַעֲנִי, אָז בָּאָרֶץ.

Abram is called Hebrew for two reasons: first, he is the descendant of Eber; second, he crossed over to the other side.

After God took the children of Israel out of Egypt and led them through the wilderness for forty years, He renewed the covenant with the next generation of Israelites. Here is what Moses says to the people:

"…that you may enter into covenant with the Lord your God, and into His oath, which the Lord your God makes with you today…" (Deuteronomy 21:11)	לְעָבְרְךָ, בִּבְרִית יְהוָה אֱלֹהֶיךָ--וּבְאָלָתוֹ: אֲשֶׁר יְהוָה אֱלֹהֶיךָ, כֹּרֵת עִמְּךָ הַיּוֹם.

The Hebrew text does not say "enter" but "crossing over," using the verb עבר. The entire Hebrew nation is "crossing over" into the covenant with God. If you just "enter," you can exit easily, but when you "cross over" you find yourself more permanently on the other side. In this case it is God's side.

Isaiah calls Abraham the father of Hebrew people:

"Look to Abraham your father, and to Sarah who bore you; for I called him alone, and blessed him and increased him." (Isaiah 51:2 NKJ)

In Galatians 3:29, all, including the nations who have faith in the Messiah, are called Abraham's seed, and they inherit the promises. Could it be that someone who is not Jewish but crosses over to the God who is called "the God of Hebrews" (Exodus 7:16) also has the status of being Hebrew?

In Ephesians 2, we learn that the nations become part of the commonwealth of Israel. They do not replace Israel; they are added to the kingdom of God, which began with Israel. They join together with the Jewish people and form an entity called "one new man." A person does not have to be Jewish to be part of God's Israel.

As we'll see, the emergence of one new man is a vital part of the foundation of God's kingdom.

8
Abraham and Ruth

Earlier, we looked at Isaiah 51:2:

> "Look to Abraham your father, and to Sarah who bore you; for I called him alone, and blessed him and increased him." (Isa 51:2 NKJ)

Scripture encourages us to look to Abraham our father and Sarah our mother. What can we learn by looking at their lives? Let's turn our attention to Abraham, who is called our father because God said to him that he would become a father of many nations.

Scripture gives us very little information about the early years of Abraham's life. Before the famous *Lech – Lecha* in Genesis 12, there are a few verses in Genesis 11 that introduce us to Abraham's father, Terah:

> This *is* the genealogy of Terah: Terah begot Abram, Nahor, and Haran. Haran begot Lot. And Haran died before his father Terah in his native land, in Ur of the Chaldeans. Then Abram and Nahor took wives: the name of Abram's wife *was* Sarai, and the name of Nahor's wife, Milcah, the daughter of Haran

the father of Milcah and the father of Iscah. But Sarai was barren; she had no child. (Genesis 11:27-30)

We read that Terah had three sons: Abram, Nahor, and Haran. But Sarai was barren; she had no child.

So what do we learn here? Haran dies young – prematurely. Nahor marries Milcha, the daughter of his brother, Haran, who died. Abram marries Sarai. Sarai happens to be barren. In the verses that follow, we learn that Terah takes his family to Canaan. For some reason, they stop half way and change their mind about continuing to their destination.

Is there a connection between all these statements? What is behind this story? Why do they go to Canaan and then change their mind and end up staying somewhere else? And all this happens before God calls Abram to go from his father's house.

First, I want to ask why is Nahor, Abraham's brother, marrying his niece, Milcha? Could it be that it is a prototype of *yebbum*? The law of *yebbum* (Hebrew ייבום) is the form of marriage found in the Bible. As specified by Deuteronomy 25:5–10, the brother of a man who died without children must marry the widow, so that the name of the deceased will not be blotted out of Israel. It is an act of kindness to give the brother a legacy that he can no longer give to himself because he is dead. In the case of Nahor, it is not quite the same; he is marring his niece and not the wife of Haran. Also Haran already has children, but it looks like it might be the same idea: to give the brother a child which would give him a greater legacy. This is an act of kindness to the brother, a true expression of brotherly love. It's also worth mentioning that the meaning of the name Milcha is "queen."

ABRAHAM AND RUTH

My next question is this: who is Iscah? It says she is the daughter of Haran. But the name appears only this one time in the whole Bible. Can we learn anything about her? In Genesis 20, Abraham tells King Abemalech about his wife, Sarah:

> "But indeed *she is* truly my sister. She *is* the daughter of my father, but not the daughter of my mother; and she became my wife." (Genesis 20:12 NKJ)

We learn here that Sarah is Abraham's half-sister.

In Biblical terms, the word father can also refer to a grandfather, and a sister can also be a niece. What is interesting that the root of the word יסכה (*Iscah*) relates to the word נסיך (*nasich*) which means prince (Joshua 13:21, Psalm 83:12). So Iscah is a princess.

The Jewish sages in the Middle Ages concluded that Iscah is Sarah, though some Christian scholars disagree. Nevertheless, it makes sense that Iscah was called Sarai by Abram, which means: "my princess." And later God changes her name to Sarah as He also changes Abram to Abraham.

Here is what Rashi[1] wrote in his Genesis commentary hundreds of years ago.

> Iscah is Sarah because [...] יִסְכָּה is an expression denoting princedom, [...] just as Sarah is an expression of dominion (שְׂרָרָה). [from Meg. 14a]

---

1 Shlomo Yitzchaki (Hebrew: רבי שלמה יצחקי; Latin: Salomon Isaacides; French: Salomon de Troyes, 22 February 1040 – 13 July 1105), today generally known by the acronym Rashi, was a medieval French rabbi and author of a comprehensive commentary on the Talmud and commentary on the Hebrew Bible (the Tanakh).

So, Abram, like his brother Nahor, is also marrying the daughter of the brother who died. Both brothers want to bless Haran, who died, with a greater legacy.

Now the following statement makes more sense. "But Sarai was barren; she had no child" (Genesis 11:30).

While Nahor succeeded in having children and being able to bless his brother, Abram could not because Sarai was barren.

The next thing we read in the story is that Terah, the father, takes the family, and they travel to the land of Canaan. So they travel to the same place where God will later call Abram out of Haran (see Genesis 12:4). For some reason, Abram's father took the whole family on a journey toward Canaan, stopping at the city of Haran.[2] Suddenly they abandoned their goal and decided to stay there permanently:

| And Terah took his son Abram and his grandson Lot, the son of Haran, and his daughter-in-law Sarai, his son Abram's wife, and they went out with them from Ur of the Chaldeans to go to the land of Canaan; and they came to Haran and dwelt there. (Genesis 11:31 NKJ) | וַיִּקַּח תֶּרַח אֶת־אַבְרָם בְּנוֹ, וְאֶת־לוֹט בֶּן־הָרָן בֶּן־בְּנוֹ, וְאֵת שָׂרַי כַּלָּתוֹ, אֵשֶׁת אַבְרָם בְּנוֹ; וַיֵּצְאוּ אִתָּם מֵאוּר כַּשְׂדִּים, לָלֶכֶת אַרְצָה כְּנַעַן, וַיָּבֹאוּ עַד־חָרָן, וַיֵּשְׁבוּ שָׁם. |

This phrase: וַיֵּשְׁבוּ שָׁם, and dwelt there, means that they stayed permanently. Their sights are no longer set on Canaan.

---

2 Haran the city is not related to Haran, the brother of Abram. The first letter of the brother's name is ה whereas the first letter of the city's name is ח.

This phrase appears in Hebrew only a few times. The phrase first appears a few verses earlier. There we read about the people who came to the land of Shinar. The land of Shinar is where Nimrod began to build his kingdom, starting with Babel (Gen. 10:10).

And it came to pass, as they journeyed from the east, that they found a plain in the land of Shinar, and they dwelt there. (Genesis 11:2 NKJ)	וַיְהִי, בְּנָסְעָם מִקֶּדֶם; וַיִּמְצְאוּ בִקְעָה בְּאֶרֶץ שִׁנְעָר, וַיֵּשְׁבוּ שָׁם.

There they began to build a city and a tower. They were afraid of being scattered and hoped to make a name for themselves. But in the end, they got scattered anyway. As I mentioned in chapter 5, if we spend all our energy and talents to promote our own name, we also become like tower-builders and lose ourselves. On the other hand, people do care about their legacy because it is important. But the question is: do we use the talents and abilities God gave us to promote ourselves or somebody else? God did take care of Abraham's legacy. So the phrase, "and they stayed there," (וַיֵּשְׁבוּ שָׁם) is somehow connected to the fear of losing the family name, a fear of disappearing forever.

Later we find this phrase in the book of Ruth. There we learn about a family from Israel that left Bethlehem – a father, a mother, and two sons. They left Bethlehem because of the famine and went to Moab. In Moab the father died, and the two sons married Moabite women.

Now they took wives of the women of Moab: the name of the one was Orpah, and the name of the other Ruth. And they *dwelt there* about ten years.	וַיִּשְׂאוּ לָהֶם, נָשִׁים מֹאֲבִיּוֹת-שֵׁם הָאַחַת עָרְפָּה, וְשֵׁם הַשֵּׁנִית רוּת; **וַיֵּשְׁבוּ שָׁם**, כְּעֶשֶׂר שָׁנִים

This family was also about to lose their name and their legacy after the father and both sons died. All the men had disappeared from the family. The rest of the story shows how Ruth was used to restore Elimelech's name. The life of Ruth is closely connected to the life of Abraham. Here is an amazing verse:

> And Boaz answered and said to her, "It has been fully reported to me, all that you have done for your mother-in-law since the death of your husband, and *how you have left your father and your mother and the land of your birth, and have come to a people whom you did not know before."* (Ruth 2:11 NKJ)

Compare this to what God said to Abram in Genesis 12:1:

> "Go from your country, *and from your relatives and from your father's house,* to the land which I will show you;"

Boaz honors Ruth for being willing to leave her father's land, house, and people to dwell with a people she did not know. Likewise, Boaz admires the kindness Ruth has shown to Naomi.

ABRAHAM AND RUTH

Here we find a striking similarity between Abraham and Ruth: both are involved in acts of kindness. Abraham wants to enlarge his brother's inheritance, and Ruth is restoring the legacy of Elimilech's family. We will look closer at the life of Ruth in the next chapter.

So, Sarai is barren, and the family sets out on a quest to the land of Canaan. Why to the land of Canaan? Maybe they thought that Canaan was the holy land, and they went there so see if Sarai would get pregnant. Whatever the reason, when the family reached Haran, they abandoned their mission and stayed there. Something happened to Abram in Haran. He may have had doubts and fears. His wife was barren, and he was probably thinking: "I cannot give my brother a child, and what about me, my name, my legacy?" Perhaps he even thought about abandoning Sarai. In any event, they put their roots in Haran.

This is somewhat complicated. So, I will explain one more time. This phrase, "and stayed there," is thematically connected in various parts of the Scripture to the loss of legacy by permanently settling in a specific place. This tells me that the family of Abram made their move from the city of Ur with a specific mission that was abandoned. Abram was about to become a tower builder. But…

But God saw something here. He saw that while much of humanity was scattered because they tried to save their own name by building the tower, there was one man who cared about the name of his brother. By seeking to perpetuate the name of his brother and not his own, perhaps he will perpetuate God's name. So God comes to Abram here, in Haran, not in Ur and tells him: "לך-לך" – "Go…." Why Haran and not Ur? Because the next verse says:

> So Abram went *away* as the Lord had spoken to him; and Lot went with him. Now Abram was seventy-five years old when he departed from Haran. (Gen 12:4)

So Abram goes to the land of Canaan, and there he lives in tents, not in houses. He does not build a tower but instead the altars where he calls on the name of God. He begins to perpetuate God's name in the land of promise.

Thus the love of one's brother is the foundation of the kingdom of God:

> If someone says, "I love God," and hates his brother, he is a liar; for he who does not love his brother whom he has seen, how can he love God whom he has not seen? And this commandment we have from Him: that he who loves God *must* love his brother also. (1 John 4:20-21 NKJ)

Elsewhere we read about conflicts between brothers: Isaac and Ishmael, Jacob and Esau, Josef and his brothers. But in the end, they all found a way to reconcile. The kingdom of God is built on brotherly love.

Because Abram cared about his brother's name and then began to perpetuate God's name, God promised to take care of Abram's name:

> I will make you a great nation; I will bless you and make your name great; and you shall be a blessing. (Genesis 12:2 NKJ)

ABRAHAM AND RUTH

One more thing worth mentioning here relates to the family of Terah. Terah had three sons, Abram, Nahor, and Haran. Through Abraham and Sarah, our forefathers were born, Isaac, Jacob, and the founders of the twelve tribes of Israel. At the same time, we have our foremothers from Nahor, Rebecca, Leah, and Rachel.

The brother who died, Haran, had a son whose name was Lot. Lot later had a son whose name was Moab. Moab became the father of the Moabites. Ruth was a Moabite. So, Ruth is a descendent of Haran, which makes her part of the family of Terah. Abram showed kindness to his brother Haran. Centuries later, Abram's descendants, the family of Elimelech, were about to lose their legacy. Then, a descendant of Haran, Ruth, showed kindness to the family of Elimelech, thus returning the kindness shown by Abram, who once blessed her forefather. She completed the circle and paved the way for the promise given to Abraham by God:

"I will make you exceedingly fruitful, and I will make nations of you, and *kings will come from you.*" (Genesis 17:6)

This is also what God promised to Jacob:

"I am God Almighty; be fruitful and multiply; a nation and a multitude of nations shall come from you, and *kings shall come from you.*" (Genesis 35:11)

And, as we'll see, from Ruth's courage and faithfulness, a son is born, Boaz, the father of King David. King David is the fulfilment of the prophesies given to Abraham and Jacob. Then from the line of David comes the Messiah, the King Himself, who will rule over the entire world.

9
Ruth

In this chapter, I would like to take an even a deeper look at the life of Ruth. Her background begins with the story of Lot, Abraham's nephew. In Genesis 19, God sends two angels to rescue Lot and his family before two cities, Sodom and Gomorrah, are destroyed. In the process of escaping, Lot loses his wife, who turns into a pillar of salt. At the end of their flight, Lot and his two daughters end up living in a cave on the side of a mountain. After witnessing the destruction of Sodom and Gomorrah, the daughters of Lot think that there is no man left on earth to continue their family lineage:

> Now the firstborn said to the younger, "Our father *is* old, and *there is* no man on the earth to come in to us as is the custom of all the earth." (Genesis 19:31 NKJ)

Seeing no other means to extend their family line, the daughters ply their father with wine and then each sleeps with him. The plan works. Both daughters are impregnated. The older daughter gives birth to a son named Moab (מואב -- *moav* in Hebrew). In time he becomes the father of an eponymous nation, Moab, which means "from the father." Having its genesis in incest, Moab's power is one of seduction.

In Numbers 22 we read that when the Israelites were on their journey from Egypt, the king of Moab hired the prophet Balaam to curse them. But a problem arose. When Balaam opened his mouth to pronounce a curse, a blessing would emerge instead. So the king of Moab changed his strategy. He instructed the Moabite women to seduce Israelite men, and to entice them to them to worship their deity, Baal Peor. When the anger of God turned on the children of Israel, 24,000 people were slain. Consequently, laws were written in the Torah against the Moabites:

> An Ammonite or Moabite shall not enter the assembly of the LORD; even to the tenth generation none of his *descendants* shall enter the assembly of the LORD forever, because they did not meet you with bread and water on the road when you came out of Egypt, and because they hired against you Balaam the son of Beor from Pethor of Mesopotamia, to curse you. Nevertheless the LORD your God would not listen to Balaam, but the LORD your God turned the curse into a blessing for you, because the LORD your God loves you. You shall not seek their peace nor their prosperity *all your days forever*. (Deuteronomy 23:3-6 NKJ)

Interestingly, generations later, a Moabite woman, Ruth, is used by God to change the course of history. The story of Ruth begins with an Israelite family leaving Bethlehem because of a famine. Bethlehem was a major town in the territory of Judah. The full name of the town was Bethlehem Ephrathah. Ephrathah means "fruitful," and Bethlehem means "house of bread." So no bread (or fruit or food of any kind) was to be found in the house of bread.

Elimelech takes his wife and his two children to Moab in search of a better life. Elimelech comes from a prominent and very influential family. But in time of trouble, he forsakes his people to save himself and his family. The name Elimelech means "My God is king." There is a symbolic message here: God has departed from Israel.

This story takes place in the period of judges when Israel had no human king. But there was a King in Israel – God. Israel was the kingdom of God on the Earth. But now it looks like the nation is forsaken by their King.

Elimelech's wife was Naomi, whose name means "pleasant." The names of their sons were Mahlon and Chilion. Mahlon means "sickness," and Chilion means "destruction." After living in Moab for some time, Elimelech, the father, died. Naomi's two sons married local Moabite women, another act of disobedience. After ten years of living in Moab, Mahlon and Chilion died as well. After this, Naomi heard that the famine had ended in Bethlehem. So she made the decision to go back home to the land of Judah. As she went, both of her daughters-in-law declared they wanted to go with her. But Naomi tried to discourage them:

> And Naomi said to her two daughters-in-law, "Go, return each to her mother's house. The LORD deal kindly with you, as you have dealt with the dead and with me." (Ruth 1:8 NKJ)

Still, Naomi's daughters-in-law insisted:

> And they said to her, "Surely we will return with you to your people." (Ruth 1:10 NKJ)

As we'll see, this story is rich with prophetic symbolism. Naomi's family represents Israel going into exile as the result of their disobedience to God. The nation of Israel went through two exiles, with persecution and antisemitism resulting in the death of many. During the last exile, one of the most horrific events that the Jewish people experienced was the Holocaust. The Lord warned what would happen in the exile, as we read in the book of Leviticus:

> You shall perish among the nations, and the land of your enemies shall eat you up. (Leviticus 26:38 NKJ)

Of course, God doesn't place all the blame on the Jewish people. The prophet Zechariah says:

> "I am exceedingly angry with the nations at ease;
> For I was a little angry, and they helped—*but* with evil *intent*." (Zechariah 1:15 NKJ)

The nations oppressed the Jewish people for their own evil purposes. And the Lord promised to deal with the nations that oppressed Israel. Later, Zechariah—along with other prophets—declared that God would eventually bring the Jewish people back to the land of Israel before the return of the Messiah.

The time for the Jews to return to the land has begun! Just like Naomi returned to the land, so the Jewish people have now begun to return to the Land of Israel. The migration started in 1882 – the year when Aliyah[1] began. And it is still continuing. In 1948, Israel once again became a nation.

Similarly in Ruth, Naomi, who lost her family, is going back home. Why would these two young Moabite women want to go with her to a place they had never been and to a nation with a very different culture? Perhaps being married to two Israelis for ten years and living with an Israelite family allowed them to learn something about the God of Israel and the lifestyle of Israelites. For example, on the seventh day they would not work in the fields. Then, I think, the women would ask: "what is the reason?" They did not observe Shabbat in their Moabite culture. Even though this Israelite family lived in disobedience towards God, yet they kept their lifestyle, and the knowledge of God came to these Moabites through them. This parallels what Paul wrote to the believers in Rome:

> I say then, have they stumbled that they should fall? Certainly not! *But through their fall, to provoke them to jealousy, salvation has come to the Gentiles.* (Rom 11:11 NKJ)

In other words, God used Israel's disobedience to bring salvation to the Gentiles.

Now back to the story of Ruth. Naomi, for the second time, tells her daughters-in-law to go back:

---

[1] Aliyah is the Hebrew word which describes the return of the Jewish people back to the Land of Israel, out of exile. Prior to 1882 there were handful Jews living in the Land of Israel. The first immigrants came in 1882 from Romania, then later from Russia.

"Turn back, my daughters; why will you go with me? *Are* there still sons in my womb, that they may be your husbands?" (Ruth 1:11 NKJ)

After going part of the way, one of the daughters, Orpah, departs and goes back to Moab. The name "Orpha" is related to the Hebrew word עורף which means "nape" – the back of the neck. She acts out the meaning of her name by turning away and showing the back of her neck to Naomi. But Ruth, whose name means beloved friend, remains with Naomi all the way to the land of Israel.

Two women divide and go to separate directions. Why did Orpah leave? Naomi herself explains this to Ruth, entreating her to leave also:

And she said, "Look, your sister-in-law has gone back to her people and to her gods; return after your sister-in-law." (Ruth 1:15 NKJ)

When Orpah was reminded about her own people and gods, she realized that she could not fully give up her gods and serve the God of Israel. The first commandment is very clear: "You shall have no other gods besides me." Orpha could not continue because she could not give up her Moabite way of living.

Today, the body of Yeshua around the world is predominantly non-Jewish, and the majority do not have an understanding of why Israel is still important in God's plan for the establishment of the Kingdom. But there are those who understand the importance of Israel. Even among those, there is division. There are those believers who are interested in Israel but are not able to give up pagan practices. They cannot go all the way and identify fully with Israel. Orpha represents those who cannot go all the way. On the other hand, there are those who fully identify themselves with Israel and the Jewish people. Ruth represents this group of people.

This is how Ruth responds to Naomi:

> But Ruth said: "Entreat me not to leave you, or to turn back from following after you; for wherever you go, I will go; and wherever you lodge, I will lodge; Your people shall be my people, and your God, my God. Where you die, I will die, and there will I be buried. The LORD do so to me, and more also, if anything but death parts you and me." (Ruth 1:16-17 NKJ)

The part "your people shall be my people" is not translated exactly from the Hebrew. The Hebrew text says "your people are my people," which shows that Ruth already identified herself with Naomi's people. Thus, she was determined to totally leave her pagan roots and embrace the God of Israel and His people. She said to Naomi: "Where you die, I will die, and there will I be buried." She was willing to die with Naomi and her people; her whole life, her whole being is identified with the people of Israel. And so she continued with Naomi to the land of Israel. This identification is seen in the words of the relative of Naomi, Boaz, who appears in the second chapter of the book of Ruth.

| And Boaz answered and said to her, "It has been fully reported to me, all that you have done for your mother-in-law since the death of your husband, *and how you have left your father and your mother and the land of your birth*, and have come to a people whom you did not know before." (Ruth 2:11 NKJ) | וַיַּעַן בֹּעַז, וַיֹּאמֶר לָהּ--הֻגֵּד הֻגַּד לִי כֹּל אֲשֶׁר-עָשִׂית אֶת-חֲמוֹתֵךְ, אַחֲרֵי מוֹת אִישֵׁךְ; וַתַּעַזְבִי אָבִיךְ וְאִמֵּךְ, וְאֶרֶץ **מוֹלַדְתֵּךְ**, וַתֵּלְכִי, אֶל-עַם אֲשֶׁר לֹא-יָדַעַתְּ תְּמוֹל שִׁלְשׁוֹם. |

This text connects Ruth to Abraham. Compare it to what God said to Abram in Genesis 12:

| Now the LORD said to Abram, "Go from your country and your kindred and your father's house to the land that I will show you." (Genesis 12:1 ESV) | וַיֹּאמֶר יְהוָה אֶל-אַבְרָם, לֶךְ-לְךָ מֵאַרְצְךָ **וּמִמּוֹלַדְתְּךָ** וּמִבֵּית אָבִיךָ, אֶל-הָאָרֶץ, אֲשֶׁר אַרְאֶךָּ. |

Here we find a striking similarity between Abraham and Ruth: both are involved in acts of kindness. Abraham wants to enlarge his brother's inheritance, and Ruth is restoring the legacy of Elimelech's family. Both became a blessing to all mankind. It is worth mentioning that there is also a difference between these passages. The Lord told Abraham to leave his father's house, whereas Boaz reminded Ruth how she left her father and mother. This connects Ruth to what is said in Genesis 2:

> Therefore a man shall leave his father and mother and be joined to his wife, and they shall become one flesh. (Genesis 2:24 NKJ)

Adam and Eve started a new foundation – family. Ruth represents a new foundation where the nations and Israel become one family in the Lord.

Let's get back to our story. Symbolically, Naomi represents Israel in exile, but now she is going back home. During recent decades, many Jews have made Aliyah. Many Jewish families lost their loved ones during the Holocaust, in various wars, and through terrorist acts. They are like Naomi, feeling the pain of loss. When Naomi came back to Israel she said: "Do not call me Naomi, but call me Marah," which means "bitter." It's fair to say the majority of Israelites today carry this generational and historical pain. And as biblical Ruth was instrumental in the restoration of the life and legacy of Naomi, I believe that there is a modern-day-Ruth who is able to heal the wounded hearts of the people of Israel and restore their true call.

I have lived in Israel for more than ten years, and I began to see modern-day Ruth coming to bless the people of Israel with love and kindness and the healing power of the Holy Spirit. She is coming from Germany, Holland, Finland, England, USA, China, Hong Kong, Malaysia, and from many more countries around the world. Of course, these are believers in Yeshua who have their hearts connected to Israel and believe that the restoration of Israel leads to the establishment of the kingdom of God in the world.

It is important to understand why Ruth received such kindness in Israel. Earlier we read that Moabites were excluded from being blessed by the Law in the Torah. But when Boaz and Ruth met, he showed her kindness. I am sure that Boaz knew about the law, yet he went out of his way to bless her. I think he understood something deeper. First of all, Boaz had good reason to identify with a foreigner. His mother, Rahab, is listed in the genealogy in Matthew 1. Her name is Rahab. She was a harlot who spied for the Israelites before they conquered Jericho. Though not an Israelite, Rahab was given a full place in the nation.

Yes, there is the law that prohibits the Moabites from worshipping within Israel, but there is another law that balances it all. It is the law of mercy:

> Mercy and truth have met together; Righteousness and peace have kissed. (Psalm 85:10 NKJ, verse 11 in Hebrew Bible)

The truth is the Word of God, the laws of God. And the law was against Ruth and the entire Moabite nation. If God acted on truth alone, none of us would have a chance, for we have all fallen short of the glory of God, as Paul stated in his letter to the believers in Rome. But God balances truth with mercy. The Hebrew word used here is חֶסֶד *(chesed)*, and it means mercy, grace, a gift of kindness that carries a power of God's love for people to be received by Him. *Chesed* (mercy) has the power to heal people's hearts. In the gospel of John, Yeshua is described as somebody who is full of grace and truth.

This word for mercy is one of the key words in the book of Ruth. Ruth receives kindness, and now she is giving it to her mother-in-law, Naomi. Through God's mercy, the nations have something to give back to the Jewish people, as Paul said in the letter to the believers in Rome:

> For as you (Gentiles) were once disobedient to God, yet have now obtained mercy through their (Jews) disobedience, even so these also have now been disobedient, that through the mercy shown you they also may obtain mercy. (Romans 11:30-31 NKJ)

People can't give what they don't have. But when the gift from God is received, we have something to give to others. Ruth received a gift from God, the gift of kindness. So did the nations that came to the God of Israel. They came by the way of mercy and joined the covenant that God made with Israel. Yes, the new covenant is made with Israel:

> Behold, the days are coming, says the Lord, when I will make a new covenant with the house of Israel and with the house of Judah. (Jeremiah 31:31)

According to Jeremiah, the new covenant is promised to Israel and Judah. There is no separate covenant with the nations. Yeshua made a way for the nations to join this covenant through God's grace and mercy. If you are a believer in Yeshua today, you have received God's gift of love. What will you be doing with your gift?

At the beginning of Romans 12, Paul says this:

> I beseech you therefore, brethren, by the mercies of God, that you present your bodies a living sacrifice, holy, acceptable to God, *which is* your reasonable service. (Romans 12:1, NKJ)

Paul is saying this after his statement in chapter 11 about Gentiles showing the mercy of God to the people of Israel. Ruth is the best example of what it means to be a living sacrifice to God. She was purely motivated by love. She came to the people of Naomi risking rejection for being a Moabitess. She totally changed the direction of her life and associated herself with the people of Israel. Not only was she able to heal the heart of Naomi, but she did much more. She was used to restore the name of the family of Elimelech and paved the way for the throne of David to become a reality. It is to King David that the promise is made of an eternal throne with the true king, the Messiah, sitting on it forever. Thus, Ruth became a divine connection for the establishment of the Eternal Kingdom.

Besides this, I believe Ruth, through her faithfulness, removed the curse that had been on the Moabites. In chapter 3, Naomi tells Ruth to put on a beautiful garment, to anoint herself and go to the field at night. She is to wait until Boaz has eaten and drunk, so his heart will become happy. When he lies down to sleep, she is to lie down at his feet.

This happened before in the ancestry of Ruth. Her forefather Lot became drunk. His two daughters slept with him, thus founding the Moabite nation. Did Naomi realize what a dangerous situation she was sending Ruth into? A Moabitess whose nation was powerful in seduction. The same scenario is repeated: a Moabitess at the feet of a drunken man. The daughters of Lot wanted a continuation of mankind. Ruth wanted to restore the continuation of Elimelech's family. Like her ancestors, Ruth could have resorted to seduction, but she chose the way of righteousness instead.

Ruth went and laid at the feet of Boaz after he ate and drank and his heart was merry and happy. He was asleep, and when he woke up, he saw a woman lying at his feet. He startled and asked her: "Who are you?" Ruth revealed herself to Boaz, and instead of seducing him she challenged him to stand up to what was right. Boaz had said earlier that God had taken Ruth under his wings (Ruth 2:12). And now it is his role to take her under his, so to speak.

Ruth was lying under Boaz's garment, which is called a tallit. There are fringes that are attached to the corners of this garment. These corners are called כנפיים *(k'nafaim)*, which means "wings." Thus his garment is the symbol of Boaz becoming the covering for Ruth.

Boaz himself had issues in his ancestry. His fore-mother was Tamar (Genesis 38 – read the story of Judah and Tamar). She also wanted to save the legacy of her late husband. She did it in a noble but not very kosher way. Boaz, her descendant, acted in righteous way and thus also cleared his ancestry from sin.

Thus, Boaz and Ruth both cleared the way for the eternal throne of David.

Boaz married Ruth, and they had a child whose name was Obed (*Oved* in Hebrew), which means "servant." The child was given to Naomi, who nursed him. This child became a continuation of Naomi's family. Thus Ruth brought revival to Israel. Obed later had a son named Jesse, who became the father of King David. So, Ruth was responsible for the throne of David becoming a reality.

Today, when we look at modern Israel, back from exile, we see many wounded people like Naomi – feeling more bitter than

The Hidden Elephant

pleasant. As I said, I believe that the modern-day Ruth already exists. I personally have seen her function here in Israel. She came from different nations, including Germany, a country that 70 years ago tried to eliminate the Jewish nation. She is totally motivated by love. She is not interested to impose foreign religion on the Israelite people. She is interested in healing their hearts and bringing Israel to its destiny. Of course, there are nations saying: Let the name of Israel be no more, just as it is written in Psalm 83:5. But this Ruth has fully identified herself with the people of Israel. She has separated from Orpha, her sister, and sees herself with the people of the kingdom. She loves to be with them and celebrate their holidays, and she is willing to give her life for the cause of the kingdom.

A young family moved to Israel from Germany. They came as volunteers to work with Holocaust survivors. In one of the meetings I participated in, the young man lifted his guitar and kindly asked the people if he could sing a song in German. I got really concerned, thinking: "Doesn't he realize what kind of memories this language will bring up in the Holocaust survivors?" But their reaction astounded me. They smiled at him and welcomed him to sing the song in his native tongue. This young man had won their hearts, and he brought healing to their hearts. They were able to listen to this song in German without hearing the voices that wanted to sentence them to death.

Earlier, we read Isaiah 52:7: "Tell to Zion: Your king reigns." I believe that the modern-day Ruth will be able to fulfill this promise. If Biblical Ruth cleared the way for throne of David to become a reality, could it be that the modern-day Ruth will cause the throne of David to return to Jerusalem? I believe that Ruth is one of the major keys to the restoration of Israel and the return of the King.

I have a question for you: Which of the two ways will you chose? The way of Orpha or the way of Ruth? Just know that the way of Ruth may cost you everything. Remember what Ruth said to Naomi: "Where you die, I will die." Are you willing to die with the people of Israel?

10
Salvation

Salvation is one of the central messages of the kingdom story. What can we learn about salvation from Tanakh (the Old Testament)? There are two main words that are used for salvation: יְשׁוּעָה *yeshuah* and הַצָּלָה *hatzalah*. The following passage contains an instance of *yeshuah*:

> Sing to the LORD, bless His name; proclaim the good news of His salvation from day to day. (Psalm 96:2 NKJ)

> שִׁירוּ לַיהוָה בָּרֲכוּ שְׁמוֹ בַּשְּׂרוּ מִיּוֹם־לְיוֹם **יְשׁוּעָתוֹ**׃

And here is an example of *hatzalah*:

> Deliver me from the sword, my precious *life* from the power of the dog. (Psalm 22:20 NKJ)

> **הַצִּילָה** מֵחֶרֶב נַפְשִׁי; מִיַּד־כֶּלֶב, יְחִידָתִי.

In another example, *yeshuah* takes a different form:

> Save me from the lion's mouth and from the horns of the wild oxen! (Psalm 22:21 NKJ)

> **הוֹשִׁיעֵנִי**, מִפִּי אַרְיֵה; וּמִקַּרְנֵי רֵמִים עֲנִיתָנִי.

The exodus from Egypt is a great story to understand salvation. There is an episode in chapter 2 where Moses is running away to the wilderness after killing an Egyptian man. In the wilderness, he encounters the daughters of a Midian priest, who came to draw water from the well. Then some shepherds come, push the women away, and take over the well. When Moses sees what happened, he defends the young women:

> Then the shepherds came and drove them away; but Moses stood up and helped them, and watered their flock. (Exodus 2:17 NKJ)

In English we read that Moses helped the young women. But in Hebrew it says that Moses saved them:

וַיָּבֹאוּ הָרֹעִים, וַיְגָרְשׁוּם; וַיָּקָם מֹשֶׁה **וַיּוֹשִׁעָן**, וַיַּשְׁקְ אֶת-צֹאנָם.

Moses drove the shepherds away and even watered the flock. What a powerful picture of how God provides for His people when He saves them.

Next Moses is invited to the house of a Midian priest, Jethro (also Reuel), and in time he marries his daughter Zipporah. Here we have a picture of a savior marrying the one he has just saved.

The next time we meet Jethro is after the children of Israel come out of Egypt:

> And Jethro, the priest of Midian, Moses' father-in-law, heard of all that God had done for Moses and for Israel His people—that the Lord had brought Israel out of Egypt. (Exodus 18:1 NKJ)

SALVATION

So, Jethro takes Zipporah, Moses's wife, and his two sons, Gershom and Eliezer, and goes to the wilderness where the camp of the children of Israel was, at Mount Zion. There Moses and his father-in-law meet. Moses tells Jethro what he has already heard, but in a different way.

> And Moses told his father-in-law all that the Lord had done to Pharaoh and to the Egyptians for Israel's sake, all the hardship that had come upon them on the way, and *how* the Lord had delivered them. (Exodus 18:8 NKJ)

And this is Jethro's response:

> Then Jethro rejoiced for all the good which the Lord had done for Israel, whom He had delivered out of the hand of the Egyptians. And Jethro said, "Blessed *be* the Lord, who has delivered you out of the hand of the Egyptians and out of the hand of Pharaoh, *and* who has delivered the people from under the hand of the Egyptians. Now I know that the Lord *is* greater than all the gods; for in the very thing in which they behaved proudly, *He was* above them." (Exodus 18:9-11 NKJ)

Why does Jethro rejoice and bless the Lord after hearing this a second time from Moses? And more than that, he acknowledges that there is no one greater than the Lord. The first time he heard that the Lord had brought Israel out of Egypt, he was prompted to seek out Moses. But the second time he hears something startling from Moses. He hears that the Lord had saved His people.

It is one thing to usher His people to a new land, but it is another thing to save them. This shows that the most powerful being in the universe, the Creator of the world, cares about this people. He loves them. Jethro himself becomes a believer in the God of Israel.

In this story the savior, Moses, marries the one he has saved. But now it is God, the true Savior, who is marrying His people, whom he saved from the bondage of Egypt.

Salvation means being taken out of one place and brought to another. The children of Israel were brought out – saved – from slavery. Their destination is the Promised Land. But that is just on one, simple level. A deeper level is described in Exodus 19:

> "You have seen what I did to the Egyptians, and *how* I bore you on eagles' wings and brought you to Myself." (Exodus 19:4 NKJ)

The Creator of the Universe loves his people; He saves them out of slavery and brings them to Himself. The ultimate destination out of slavery is God. And that is true for all of us.

And then, after being saved, God gives them a mission:

> "Now therefore, if you will indeed obey My voice and keep My covenant, then you shall be a special treasure to Me above all people; for all the earth *is* Mine. And you shall be to Me a kingdom of priests and a holy nation." These *are* the words which you shall speak to the children of Israel. (Exodus 19:5-6 NKJ)

Here the Lord enters into the covenant with His people, whom He just saved. They become a kingdom of priests.

SALVATION

God's priest is one who teaches others about God and His values. Israel is called the first-born son. What is the role of the first-born in the family? The first born is the one who learns about his parents. His role is to teach the other children about their parents' values. Israel's role is to teach other nations about God, the Creator of the Universe, and His values.

What does it mean to be a holy nation? The phrase הַגּוֹי הַקָדוֹשׁ *(hagoy hakadosh)* rendered *kadosh*, literally means dedication. God separates his people and dedicates them, first to Himself, and then to His mission on Earth.

When we are saved, we are saved to God. And in Him we receive the mission to tell others about Him.

Yeshua's name is derived from the word יְשׁוּעָה *(yeshuah)* which means salvation. One of His chief missions is to bring salvation to the people of Israel and ultimately to the whole world. In Matthew, an angel tells Miriam (Mary) what to name her baby:

> And she will bring forth a Son, and you shall call His name Jesus (Yeshua), for He will save His people from their sins. (Mathew 1:21 NKJ)

What does Jesus have to do with saving people? When we look at the original Hebrew text (and there is evidence that the gospel of Matthew was written in Hebrew and not in Greek[1]), the

---

1 It is interesting that there has been a document discovered 20-30 years ago which some scholars believe to be an original gospel of Matthew in Hebrew and there are numerous analyses that support the theory that the gospel of Matthew had been originally written in Hebrew and not in Greek. One of the books with research has been published with the name "Hebrew Gospel of Matthew" by George Howard from the University of Georgia. He analyses the text of Matthew along an old version called Shem-Tob's Matthew.

passage looks like this:

ותקרא שמו **ישוע** כי הוא **יושיע** את עמי מעונותם

The English transliteration reads like this: "*Vetikra shemo Yeshua ki hu yoshia et ami meavonotam.*" This means: "And you will call his name Yeshua for he will save my people from their iniquities." Here it is easy to see how the name Yeshua relates to the word for salvation: *Yeshua yoshia* -- Yeshua will save.

Yeshua's salvation both frees us from past wrongdoings and gives us the power to overcome the sin that has dominated our lives since the time of Adam and Eve.

Paul, in the book of Romans, teaches us that the Gospel is power:

> For I am not ashamed of the gospel of Christ, for it is the power of God to salvation for everyone who believes, for the Jew first and also for the Greek. (Romans 1:16 NKJ)

And this is what Paul says about salvation:

> But God be thanked that *though* you were slaves of sin, yet you obeyed from the heart that form of doctrine to which you were delivered. And having been set free from sin, you became slaves of righteousness. (Romans 6:17-18 NKJ)

In other words, it is through the journey away from slavery to sin that we become righteous servants of God.

In John 3, Yeshua explains to Nicodemus that one must be born from above to see or enter the kingdom of God (John 3:3-

SALVATION

5). Salvation is a powerful, born-from-above experience that gives us entrance into the Kingdom of God. In conversation with Nicodemus, Yeshua reveals this:

> Jesus answered and said to him, "Most assuredly, I say to you, unless one is born again,[2] he cannot see the kingdom of God." Nicodemus said to Him, "How can a man be born when he is old? Can he enter a second time into his mother's womb and be born?" Jesus answered, "Most assuredly, I say to you, unless one is born of water and the Spirit, he cannot enter the kingdom of God." (John 3:3-5 NKJ)

And here are Yeshua's most famous words to Nicodemus:

> "For God so loved the world that He gave His only begotten Son, that whoever believes in Him should not perish but have everlasting life." (John 3:16 NKJ)

Clearly, salvation functions on two levels:

1. The first form of salvation is from enemy forces. Just as God saved Israel from Egypt, He will save Israel from the armies that will come against Jerusalem (Zechariah 14).
2. Second, God saves us from sin and its corrosive effects through the atonement of Yeshua. This includes individual, national, and worldwide salvation.

---

2 Better translation is born from above.

In the next chapter, we will deal with another aspect of the Kingdom of God: *shalom*.

11
Shalom

Shalom is one of four messages detailed in Isaiah 52:7. As mentioned earlier, the word *shalom* comes from the verb שָׁלֵם *(shilem)*, which means to complete. Thus, one of the meanings of the word *shalom* is completion. In modern Hebrew, this word also means to pay (*leshalem* – לְשַׁלֵּם). Yeshua, the prince of peace, paid the price for our salvation.

Let's see how this word is used in Isaiah 45:7. Starting from the last part of verse six in the New King James version:

> "I *am* the LORD, and *there is* no other; I form the light and create darkness, I make peace and create calamity." (Isaiah 45:7a NKJ)

The King James version says it differently:

> "I *am* the LORD, and *there is* none else. I form the light, and create darkness: I make peace, and create evil:" (Isa 45:7a KJV)

Is it calamity or evil? What does the Hebrew text say?

אֲנִי יְהוָה וְאֵין עוֹד: יוֹצֵר אוֹר וּבוֹרֵא חֹשֶׁךְ עֹשֶׂה שָׁלוֹם וּבוֹרֵא **רָע**
אֲנִי יְהוָה עֹשֶׂה כָל־אֵלֶּה.

The Hebrew text uses the word רע (*rah*). And this word means evil. The same word is found in the following passage:

> The Lord saw how great the wickedness of the human race had become on the earth, and that every inclination of the thoughts of the human heart was only evil all the time. (Genesis 6:5 NKJ)

Here both words, wickedness and evil, are represented by the Hebrew word רע, except "wickedness" is in the feminine form: רעה.

Does God create evil? This is not an easy question. The Hebrew word רע has a larger meaning than the English word "evil." In some situations, it can be translated as evil, like in Genesis 6:5. It also means "bad." But Isaiah 45:7 gives us another meaning. Here we have two contrasting statements. The first one is "light and darkness," where the darkness is the opposite of the light. The following line has "shalom" and "ra," where the meaning of "ra" is the opposite of shalom. If "shalom" means "completion," then the opposite of completion is incompletion. I believe the word רע here is not referring to evil the way we understand it, but rather to that which is incomplete. This understanding can help us to unlock the meanings of other passages like Genesis 2:3.

> Then God blessed the seventh day and sanctified it, because in it He rested from all His work which God had created and made. (Genesis 2:3 NKJ)

Why does the text say "created and made"? Is it not redundant? Why not just "created"? But in Hebrew it reads differently.

וַיְבָרֶךְ אֱלֹהִים אֶת־יוֹם הַשְּׁבִיעִי וַיְקַדֵּשׁ אֹתוֹ כִּי בוֹ שָׁבַת מִכָּל־מְלַאכְתּוֹ
אֲשֶׁר־**בָּרָא** אֱלֹהִים **לַעֲשׂוֹת**:

The text in Hebrew says: *barah Elohim la'asot* -- "God created to make." Not made! The word *la'asot* is in the infinitive form. To make what? Didn't God finish all his work? Yes, He did, as stated in verse two:

> By the seventh day God had *finished the work* he had been doing; so on the seventh day he rested from all his work. (Genesis 2:2 NKJ)

Most translations do not render verse three correctly. I believe that God has finished His part in full, but he left something undone, something to complete. And the completion is given to humankind.

I once heard this story:

> A pastor was invited to a farmer's house for dinner. Before dinner the farmer took the pastor to the field and showed him the wonderful corn that was growing there. "Take a look at the corn that I grew," said the farmer. The pastor, who wanted to show himself to be spiritual, said, "But God grew this corn!" "Yes, I agree with you," said the farmer. "But I also have something to do with it. Let me show you the field that God grew all by Himself!"

Here the production of corn becomes co-operation between God and man.

When God made us in His image, He gave us the ability to create. For He Himself is the Creator. The universe He created gives us an amazing opportunity for the development of technology, agriculture, and so on. As we explored earlier, God has given us the gift of creativity in order for us to partner with Him in building the Kingdom here on earth.

Incomplete creation is waiting for us to take it from the status of רע, incomplete, to the status of שלום, complete:

> For the earnest expectation of the creation eagerly waits for the revealing of the sons of God. For the creation was subjected to futility, not willingly, but because of Him who subjected it in hope; because the creation itself also will be delivered from the bondage of corruption into the glorious liberty of the children of God. For we know that the whole creation groans and labors with birth pangs together until now. (Romans 8:19 NKJ)

Sin corrupts creation:

> So God looked upon the earth, and indeed it was corrupt; for all flesh had corrupted their way on the earth. (Genesis 12:12)

We live in the post-flood world, and the creative order does not work properly. We experience bad weather patterns, such as earthquakes and hurricanes. The creation is in bondage. But Scripture indicates that the sons of God have something to do with its redemption. Who are the sons of God?

First, we need to acknowledge the Son of God, who completed His mission on the cross. These are His last words before He died:

...He said, "It is finished!" And bowing His head, He gave up His spirit. (John 19:30)

The Greek word here is: τελέω (*tel-eh'-o*). It means to bring to an end, complete, fulfill. Except Yeshua did not speak Greek, but Hebrew. In Hebrew, He said הֻשְׁלַם – (*Hushlam*) – which means completed. He made a payment to complete the transaction: to atone for our sins, to give us eternal life, and for us to become *a new creation*.

Yeshua finished His first mission, and now the sons of God are charged with completing theirs. Who are they? The answer is found in the Gospel of John:

> But as many as received Him, to them He gave the right to become children of God, to those who believe in His name: who were born, not of blood, nor of the will of the flesh, nor of the will of man, but of God. (John 1:12-13 NKJ)

Yeshua the Messiah gives us the right to be the sons of God. So, if sin corrupts the creation, what will righteousness produce? Redemption, according to Paul. What is the purpose of the sons of God? To become a house of God for His glory to dwell in. And what is God's house? This is what the angel explains to Miriam (Mary) about the birth of her baby:

> "And behold, you will conceive in your womb and bring forth a Son, and shall call His name Jesus. He will be great, and will be called the Son of the Highest; and the Lord God will give Him the throne of His father David. And He will reign over the house

of Jacob forever, and of His kingdom there will be no end." (Luke 1:31-33 NKJ)

It is the house of Jacob according to Luke. How will this house be built?

> Coming to Him *as to* a living stone, rejected indeed by men, but chosen by God *and* precious, you also, as living stones, are being built up a spiritual house, a holy priesthood, to offer up spiritual sacrifices acceptable to God through Jesus Christ. (1 Peter 2:4-5 NKJ)

The house of Jacob is the house made of living stones. In other words, God wants to live inside His people. And the believers from the nations also become part of this house to form one new man out of Jew and Gentile. Gentile is the former state of someone who becomes a believer in Yeshua. According to Ephesians 2, the believers from the nations become Israel's commonwealth and join the covenant that God made with Israel (Jeremiah 31:31).

God destroys the separation between the Jews and believers from the nations:

> For He Himself is our peace, who has made both one, and has broken down the middle wall of separation. (Ephesians 2:14 NKJ)

And here is another fulfillment of *shalom* – a ministry of reconciliation between the people and God and between Jews and the nations.

And this is how this house is built:

> Now, therefore, you are no longer strangers and foreigners, but fellow citizens with the saints and members of the household of God, having been built on the foundation of the apostles and prophets, Jesus Christ Himself being the chief corner*stone*, in whom the whole building, being fitted together, grows into a holy temple in the Lord, in whom you also are being built together for a dwelling place of God in the Spirit. (Ephesians 2:19-22 NKJ)

Here Paul is addressing the former Gentiles who became believers in the Jewish Messiah. They also became a part of the house of God together with the Jews.

So, the emergence of one new man is one of the major fulfilments of *shalom* and thus a critical step in the completion of God's house and the establishment of the Kingdom of God.

We live in the time when "Mystery Babylon" is rising in the world. It tries to impose ungodly and confusing ideas on people. It wants to take mankind into the bondage of slavery. This wicked system took Israel into two exiles. Prophet Zechariah describes this system as four horns:

> Then I raised my eyes and looked, and there *were* four horns. And I said to the angel who talked with me, "What *are* these?" So he answered me, "These *are* **the horns that have scattered Judah, Israel, and Jerusalem.**" (Zechariah 1:18-19 NKJ)

Then the prophet mentions four craftsmen who will put these horns to flight:

> Then the Lord showed me four craftsmen. And I said, "What are these coming to do?" So he said, "These *are* **the horns that scattered Judah, so that no one could lift up his head; but the craftsmen are coming to terrify them, to cast out the horns of the nations that lifted up** *their* **horn against the land of Judah to scatter it."** (Zechariah 1:20-21)

Who are these craftsmen? In Hebrew they are called חָרָשִׁים *(kharashim)*. The word literally means stone cutters. This word was applied to Bezalel, who was mentioned earlier. Bezalel is the craftsman who was building a place for God's presence in our world.

The sons of God, under the leadership of Yeshua, will defeat the wicked system, and the Kingdom of God will be established. So today we find ourselves in warfare with the kingdom of darkness. No wonder the only time the term "gospel of peace" appears in the context of spiritual warfare is in Ephesians 6:

> And having shod your feet with the preparation of (the gospel of peace. (Ephesians 6:15 NKJ

Who are the craftsmen today? They are the worshipers. Worship is the strongest weapon against the enemy. In the last days, Babylon will send armies against Jerusalem (Zechariah 14:2), and the Lord will come to fight against them. One of the ways they will be defeated is through the confusion that will come from the Lord (Zechariah 14:13). This echoes the battle that took place against Jerusalem during the days of Jehoshaphat, king of Judah (2 Chronicles 20). The Lord told the army of Judah and Jerusalem to stand still and to watch the salvation of the Lord. As they began to worship and praise the Lord in song, the confusion came on the enemy. They turned on each other and all got killed.

So when, in the last days, the armies of the nations come against Jerusalem in their attempt to prevent the establishment of the kingdom of God, I believe the worshipers will be involved in spiritual warfare, just as in the days of king Jehoshaphat. They will sing the song of the Lord. The enemy of God will be defeated, and then the Lord will establish His throne in Jerusalem – the city of peace. It can also be translated as the inheritance of peace. The Messiah of Israel, the prince of peace, will sit on this throne. Jerusalem will become the center of God's glory, and true shalom (peace) will prevail in the entire earth.

12

The Hidden Kingdom in the Scroll of Esther

There is an amazing book in the Bible known as the Esther scroll. There were many debates whether this book should have been included in the biblical canon at all. The controversy was over the fact that God is not mentioned in the entire scroll. On the surface, Esther appears to be a clever story, one often read to children in Sunday School or in synagogues during the holiday of Purim. However, on closer examination, we find a powerful, hidden story concealed within the text. The scroll of Esther unveils how God's kingdom is working from the secret place.

Even the title of the scroll, named after one of the main heroines of the book, Esther, has a dual meaning. On the one hand, it is the name of the pagan goddess Astarte. On the other, inside the word *Ester* (אֶסְתֵּר) is Hebrew word *seter* (סֵתֶר), which means "secret." Esther was a secret with a hidden identity in the pagan palace.

But who is the main character in the book of Esther? It appears to be the king, Ahasuerus. The entire first chapter is about him. Esther and her uncle Mordecai do not appear until chapter two. The king is also the focus of chapter 10:

> Now all the acts of his power and his might, and the account of the greatness of Mordecai, to which the

> king advanced him, *are* they not written in the book of the chronicles of the kings of Media and Persia? (Esther 10:2 NIJ)

The person who is mentioned here directly is the king. This phrase "are they not written in the book of chronicles" appears in 2 Kings several times. Here are a couple of examples:

> Now the rest of the acts of Amaziah, *are* they not written in the book of the chronicles of the kings of Judah? (2 Kings 14:18 NKJ)

Also:

> Now the rest of the acts of Nadab, and all that he did, *are* they not written in the book of the chronicles of the kings of Israel? (1 Kings 15:31 NKJ)

Esther is the only chronicles of Persia in the Bible. All the other instances speak about the chronicles of Judah or Israel.

The king represents the kingdom of Persia, which is continuation of a Babylonian kingdom and, in essence, is an extension of the kingdom of Nimrod. This kingdom pretends to look like the kingdom of God, but the results are the opposite. The king's palace, for example, is likened to the tabernacle, with its outer court:

> So the king said, "Who *is* in the court?" Now Haman had *just* entered the outer court of the king's palace to suggest that the king hang Mordecai on the gallows that he had prepared for him. (Esther 6:4)

There is also an inner court (Ester 5:1). Just like in the tabernacle of God, one cannot enter into the inner court of the king's palace without certain rules, or the result will be death. Here is the description of the king's court:

> And when these days were completed, the king made a feast lasting seven days for all the people who were present in Shushan the citadel, from great to small, in the court of the garden of the king's palace. There were white and blue linen curtains fastened with cords of fine linen and purple on silver rods and marble pillars; and the couches were of gold and silver on a mosaic pavement of alabaster, turquoise, and white and black marble. And they served drinks in golden vessels, each vessel being different from the other, with royal wine in abundance, according to the generosity of the king. (Esther 1:5-7 NKJ)

The colors and materials that are mentioned here clearly parallel the ones that were used in the tabernacle of God.

King Ahasuerus arranged two feasts for the princes and servants during the third year of his reign. By comparison, there was king of Israel, Solomon, who also arranged a feast for his servants in the third year of his reign. The whole story is recorded in 1 Kings 2 and 3. After the kingdom of Solomon was established, God appeared to him in a dream and said: "Ask what I shall give you." Solomon asked for a "heart that listens," 1) ,לֵב שֹׁמֵעַ Kings 3:9). This pleased God, and He gave Solomon what he asked for: a heart that understands. After Solomon awoke from his dream, he went to Jerusalem, offered burnt and peace offerings to the Lord and made a feast for all of his servants (2 Kings 2:15).

Here we see two kingdoms compared, the kingdom of Solomon, which represents God's kingdom, and the pagan kingdom of Ahasuerus. Both kings made a feast for their servants in the third year of their reign, but for different reasons. Solomon made a feast because he received a heart of understanding; whereas Ahasuerus made a feast to show the "riches of his glorious kingdom and the splendor and of his excellent majesty" (Esther 1:4).

In the course of the feasts, king Ahasuerus displays amazing generosity, serving free wine and food for everyone. By the contrast, in chapter 10, the king imposes a tax on all of the provinces and islands of the sea, so he could pay for his generosity.

On the last day of the second feast, when everyone is drunk, Ahasuerus asks his queen, Vashti, to appear before the crowd. But she refuses to enter the company of drunk men. The king gets very angry and inquires whether there is a law that would allow him to punish her. Since no such law exists, his advisors suggest to him that he create one. The new law, however, makes this issue much bigger than just the personal problem between the king and his wife. It becomes a national issue. Every woman in the kingdom must do what her husband tells her to do. If the husband asks his wife to bring him a cup of coffee, for example, and she refuses, she would be breaking the law. This pagan king creates new laws just to appease his anger. That is how the kingdom of Babylon, the kingdom of confusion, functions.

The next morning the king wakes up from being drunk and is no longer angry. He remembers what was done to Vashti. She was dismissed from being the queen and probably executed. The

THE HIDDEN KINGDOM IN THE SCROLL OF ESTHER

young men advise him to find another queen. They send messengers to all the people and provinces of the kingdom and find beautiful young virgins. These virgins are gathered into the palace and placed under the care of the king's eunuch, Hegai. There they receive treatments of oils and cosmetics for one whole year. Following that year, they will appear before the king one by one and spend a night with him, so that he will choose a new queen. The phrase used in the scroll is "gatherings of the virgins."

Here, there are a couple of connections with the story of Joseph. First, Joseph suggested to the Pharaoh that he gather grain in order to prepare for the coming famine. King Ahasuerus has a "storage" of women for whenever he would need them. Second, preparing the bodies of the women with ointment parallels Joseph preparing the body of his father, Jacob, for embalmment.

The king didn't care much about women as people. This was already evident from the way he treated Vashti and then passed the law discriminating against all women. He only cared about outward appearances.

On the appointed time, when each young woman was to go to the king, she was allowed to take with her anything she wanted according to the king's "generosity." But after spending one night with the king, the young woman couldn't go back home, even though she wasn't chosen to be the queen. She had to return to the harem, unable to see the king again unless he remembered her by name and called for her. Thus she was enslaved for the rest of her life.

We are introduced to Esther in chapter two. She had no father or mother. Thus Mordecai, her uncle, took her in as his own daughter. When the king's decree was published, she was taken into the palace and placed into the custody of Hegai. She obtained kindness and favor from him. Obeying the command of Mordecai, she did not reveal her Jewish identity to anyone in the palace.

Then the time came for Esther to be taken to the king. The text shows a difference in how Esther goes to the palace compared to the other virgins. It says, "she was taken," whereas the other virgins "went." Clearly she didn't want to be chosen. She probably couldn't imagine being the wife of a pagan king, but she gained favor in the sight of all who saw her.

The king loved Esther more than all the other women. She obtained his favor, so he made her the queen. What was the difference between Esther and the other young women? They were all beautiful. But in contrast to the others, Esther, when taken to the king, didn't take anything except for what Hegai suggested. The text doesn't tell us what she took, but it looks like she didn't just appeal to the king's eyes but to his heart. Probably for the first time in the king's life, he truly fell in love.

So why is Esther different from the others? She grew up in a Jewish home, where it was customary for fathers to bless their children. A kingdom culture would thrive in such homes, cultivated by imparting kindness, blessings, and love. After Esther's parents died, Mordecai became her father. He truly cared for her. The following verse details Mordecai's devotion to Esther:

> And every day Mordecai paced in front of the court of the women's quarters, to learn of Esther's welfare and what was happening to her. (Esther 2:11 NKJ)

Because this young woman experienced the love of a devoted father, her beauty emanated from within. She was also beautiful

THE HIDDEN KINGDOM IN THE SCROLL OF ESTHER

outwardly, but she did not need much to enhance her beauty. I wonder what Hegai told Esther to take to the king? Maybe he told her, "Just be yourself."

Today we live in a fatherless world influenced by the spirit of Nimrod, the spirit of Babylon, which is the spirit of rebellion and confusion. In our world, many daughters don't receive true affirmation and love from their fathers. They grow up insecure and dress seductively, screaming to the world "I need to be loved!"

Turning back to the text, we next learn that two men are planning to assassinate the king. This matter was revealed to Mordecai, who then informed Esther. When she told the king, the two men were apprehended and hanged.

In chapter three of the scroll, we are introduced to Haman, who was a descendant of Amalek, the grandson of Esau, an arch enemy of the Jews from ancient times.

The king promoted Haman to be the second in command in his kingdom, probably to increase security after the assassination attempt. He goes on to pass a law which requires everyone within the king's gate to bow down before Haman. Everyone obeys the law except Mordecai, who refuses. When Haman learns about this snub, he becomes filled with rage. He is further outraged when he learns that Mordecai is a Jew.

Haman goes to the pagan priests, who cast lots to determine the day when the Jews should be killed. Haman then goes to the king, suggesting that it is unprofitable for him to keep the Jews. Haman explains that the destruction of the Jews will bring the king profit. Thus an edict is passed allowing the Jews to be eradicated. The two men then celebrate with a drink. Now the king's indifference and cruelty have spread from gender to race.

When Mordecai learns about this law, he tears his cloths in grief. He communicates with Esther, pleading with her to convince the king to reverse the law. Esther reminds Mordecai that everyone within the realm knows that a death sentence awaits anyone who approaches the king unbidden. Moreover, Ester tells him that she has not been called to see the king for 30 days. Mordecai insists:

> "For if you remain completely silent at this time, relief and deliverance will arise for the Jews from another place, but you and your father's house will perish. Yet who knows whether you have come to the kingdom for *such* a time as this?" (Esther 4:14 NKJ)

In other words, the Jew's salvation isn't in Esther's hands alone. God will save them one way or another, but perhaps this is the reason she has been placed in the palace. God's name is not mentioned, but the implication is that He has chosen Esther. She is in the palace by God's providence.

Esther decides to present herself to the king. She tells Mordecai to gather all the Jews present in Shushan and instruct them to fast. They are not to eat or drink for three days. She will also do the same in the palace with her maidservants. Following three days of fasting, she will go to the king's inner chamber without being called. Just like Vashti, she will disobey the king's command. She then says these famous words: "If I perish, I perish."

By this time, Esther had been living in the palace as queen for four to five years. She likely had grown accustomed to the lavish lifestyle befitting a Persian queen. But this is her wake up call, a reminder as to which kingdom she truly belongs.

THE HIDDEN KINGDOM IN THE SCROLL OF ESTHER

Historically, Persians feasted and cast lots on the first day of each month. Haman decided this would be an apt time to destroy the Jews. So while everyone was at the palace feasting, Esther and her maidservants were fasting. In that sense, Esther was fomenting a rebellion against the kingdom of Ahasuerus already. This parallels the Day of Atonement in Israel when the lots would be cast while everyone was fasting. On this day, the high priest would go into the holiest of holies, within God's tabernacle. Similarly, Esther is about to go into the inner chamber of the pagan palace. So what happens next?

> Now it happened on the third day that Esther put on *her* royal *robes* and stood in the inner court of the king's palace, across from the king's house, while the king sat on his royal throne in the royal house, facing the entrance of the house. (Esther 5:1 NKJ)

Why do we need to know that she put on her royal robes? Obviously, she wouldn't appear in the inner court of the king in her pajamas. This must be very important. The Hebrew text provides some insight:

וַיְהִי בַּיּוֹם הַשְּׁלִישִׁי וַתִּלְבַּשׁ אֶסְתֵּר **מַלְכוּת** וַתַּעֲמֹד בַּחֲצַר בֵּית־הַמֶּלֶךְ הַפְּנִימִית וּכַח בֵּית הַמֶּלֶךְ וְהַמֶּלֶךְ יוֹשֵׁב עַל־כִּסֵּא מַלְכוּתוֹ בְּבֵית הַמַּלְכוּת נֹכַח פֶּתַח הַבָּיִת

The text provides no mention of the word "robes" or "clothes" but instead says that she puts on "kingdom" (מַלְכוּת). Of course, she puts on royal robes; that's not the question, but the text wants to take us deeper. Esther had made her choice as to which kingdom she truly belonged. Thus putting on the kingdom means that she is coming in the power of the kingdom of God. And when the kingdom of God is present, every other kingdom must bow down and kneel. Sensing Esther's new authority, king Ahasuerus, who typically reacts with vehement anger when his laws or commands are broken, extends his golden scepter toward her. Esther has once again found favor in his sight.

How does all of this apply to us now? How are we to put on the kingdom?

In Romans, Paul tells the believers to put on the Lord Yeshua HaMashiach.

> But put on the Lord Jesus Christ, and make no provision for the flesh, to *fulfill its* lusts. (Romans 13:14 NKJ)

What does it mean to put on the Lord Yeshua HaMashiach? HaMashiach means "the anointed." Who were the anointed in Israel? The kings! When we align ourselves with the kingdom of God, His presence goes with us and transforms the environment.

A few times in Israel we did concerts for holocaust survivors. Twice, during these concerts, disabled people were healed, standing up from their wheelchairs to walk. One woman hadn't walked for three years. She not only stood but began to dance! A year later, I saw her again; she was still out of the wheelchair. God's presence turns the kingdom of darkness upside down.

The book of Esther is worth rereading in light of our calling. From the moment Esther enters the king's inner chamber, the Persian world is turned upside down. Instead of the Jews being exterminated on the appointed day, the enemy is defeated. Haman is hanged on the same gallows he built for Mordecai's exe-

THE HIDDEN KINGDOM IN THE SCROLL OF ESTHER

cution. The king then grants Mordecai Haman's job and house. Talk about a reversal of fate. From this point on, the king, who formerly mistreated all women, now begins to behave gallantly towards Esther.

As mentioned earlier, God is not mentioned in the scroll. The power of the kingdom of God worked by being hidden. From an unlikely queen and acts of heroism, the entire kingdom of Babylon was transformed.

13
Judah

> Judah, you are he whom your brothers shall praise;
> Your hand shall be on the neck of your enemies;
> Your father's children shall bow down before you.
> Judah is a lion's whelp;
> From the prey, my son, you have gone up.
> He bows down, he lies down as a lion;
> And as a lion, who shall rouse him?
> The scepter shall not depart from Judah,
> Nor a lawgiver from between his feet,
> Until Shiloh comes;
> And to Him shall be the obedience of the people.
> (Genesis 49:8-10 NKJ)

This is a blessing that Jacob pronounced over Judah before his death. Shiloh is the Messiah who will come from Judah to reign over the nations.

A few centuries later God promised King David, who was from the tribe of Judah, the eternal throne:

> And your house and your kingdom shall be established forever before you. Your throne shall be established forever. (2 Samuel 7:16 NKJ)

What is special about Judah that he becomes the foundation for the eternal throne? I would have chosen Joseph. He seems like a great hero, one who saves his family and the entire nation of Egypt from famine. He went through many trials in life, but God was always with him. Many more pages in the Bible are devoted to Joseph than to Judah. So why Judah?

Judah is the one who suggested that Joseph be sold into slavery.[1] First the brothers wanted to kill Joseph. But Ruben wanted to save him and return him to the father:

> But Reuben heard it, and he delivered him out of their hands, and said, "Let us not kill him." And Reuben said to them, "Shed no blood, but cast him into this pit which is in the wilderness, and do not lay a hand on him"—that he might deliver him out of their hands, and bring him back to his father. (Genesis 37:21-22 NKJ)

Ruben was not able to convince his brothers though. Then Judah suggested they sell him:

> So Judah said to his brothers, "What profit is there if we kill our brother and conceal his blood? Come and let us sell him to the Ishmaelites, and let not our hand be upon him, for he is our brother and our flesh." And his brothers listened. (Genesis 37:26-27 NKJ)

---

[1] The author assumes that the reader has read the book of Genesis; otherwise this chapter will not make much sense.

JUDAH

The brothers listen to Judah but not Ruben. Judah already displays his leadership qualities here by being able to persuade his brothers to follow him. Unfortunately, he is leading them in the wrong direction for now.

The next time we learn more about Judah is in Genesis 38. Judah has a daughter-in-law who is married to his son Er. Er dies and Judah gives Tamar to Er's brother Onan. Onan also dies. Both brothers are killed by God for their wickedness. Then Judah tells Tamar to remain a widow until his youngest son grows up and is old enough to marry her. But for some reason, Judah delays giving Tamar to his son in marriage. Perhaps he fears that she has something to do with his other sons' deaths.

Next, Judah's wife dies. When Tamar hears that Judah is going to the sheep shearers in Timnath, she changes her garments of widowhood and dresses up as a harlot. She positions herself next to the entrance of a place called Enain. Judah sees her and, assuming that she is a harlot, asks to go in to her. She in return asks for payment. He promises to send her a young goat. She agrees but requests a deposit until the goat is received. She asks for his signet ring, cord[2] and the staff. Judah gives her the items and goes in to her. The next day he sends a goat, hoping to get his pledge back. But Tamar is nowhere to be found. She has changed her garments from those of a harlot back to those of a widow.

The items that Judah gave to Tamar as a pledge represent kingship. The signet is a ring that kings would have used to seal important documents or codify laws. The bracelet and staff also represent the authority of a king. At that time, Judah did not live

---

2 Probably a kind of bracelet.

with his family. He had a clan of his own, acting as king over them. Overcome by lust, Judah allowed his kingly regalia to be taken from him. In order to see all the parallels in the story of Tamar, we need to find out why Judah left his family? The answer is likely found at the beginning of the chapter:

It came to pass at that time that Judah departed from his brothers, and visited a certain Adullamite whose name *was* Hirah. (Genesis 38:1 NKJ)	וַיְהִי בָּעֵת הַהִוא וַיֵּרֶד יְהוּדָה מֵאֵת אֶחָיו וַיֵּט עַד־אִישׁ עֲדֻלָּמִי וּשְׁמוֹ חִירָה

The word יָרַד (*yarad*) translated here as "departed," literally means "to go down." It makes a connection to Joseph. In Genesis 39:1, we read that Joseph *was brought down* to Egypt by the Ishmaelites. The word here is הוֹרִדֻהוּ (*horiduhu*) which comes from the same root, *yarad*. So Judah's going down connects with the same word to Joseph being brought down to slavery. Another connection to both stories can be seen when the brothers come to the father to tell him about Joseph. They killed a goat and dipped Joseph's coat in its blood. Then they showed the coat to Jacob to make him think that Joseph was killed by the wild animal. There is also mention of a goat in the story of Judah. These connections give us a hint that Judah left the clan because of what happened to Joseph, seeing that Jacob could not be comforted. Judah felt guilty and could not endure his father's grief. This could be the point in time when he began to examine his heart, which will affect his responses to the events that are about to unfold.

JUDAH

After three months, Tamar shows signs that she is pregnant. Judah accuses her of adultery. He commands her to be brought before him and orders her to be executed by burning. But Tamar reveals the three items that she procured from Judah – the signet, the bracelet, and the staff. She asks him to *acknowledge* (recognize) that they are indeed his, signifying he is the father of her child.

When she *was* brought out, she sent to her father-in-law, saying, "By the man to whom these belong, I *am* with child." And she said, "Please determine (recognise) whose these *are*—the signet and cord (bracelet), and staff." (Genesis 38:25 NKJ)	הִוא מוּצֵאת, וְהִיא שָׁלְחָה אֶל־חָמִיהָ לֵאמֹר, לְאִישׁ אֲשֶׁר־אֵלֶּה לּוֹ, אָנֹכִי הָרָה; וַתֹּאמֶר, **הַכֶּר־נָא**--לְמִי הַחֹתֶמֶת וְהַפְּתִילִים וְהַמַּטֶּה, הָאֵלֶּה.

The same word "recognize" was spoken by the brothers when they brought Joseph's coat to Jacob, which was covered in goat's blood:

Then they sent the tunic of *many* colours, and they brought *it* to their father and said, "We have found this. Do you know (recognise) whether it *is* your son's tunic or not?" (Genesis 37:32 NKJ)	וַיְשַׁלְּחוּ אֶת־כְּתֹנֶת הַפַּסִּים, וַיָּבִיאוּ אֶל־אֲבִיהֶם, וַיֹּאמְרוּ, זֹאת מָצָאנוּ: **הַכֶּר־נָא**, הַכְּתֹנֶת בִּנְךָ הִוא--אִם־לֹא.

Both stories have the same word, הַכֶּר־נָא *(hakerna)*, recognize. The name Judah comes from the Hebrew verb לְהוֹדוֹת *(lechodot)*, which has two meanings. The first is "to give thanks." The second is "to acknowledge," "to admit" or "to recognize." Tamar is asking Judah not only to recognize the items but also to admit the truth. Judah, as ruler, could have covered this affair and had her executed. Nobody would have suspected his inhumanity. Instead, he chose to face the truth. He stood up to the meaning of his name:

So Judah acknowledged *them* and said, "She has been more righteous than I, because I did not give her to Shelah my son." (Genesis 38:26 NKJ)	וַיַּכֵּר יְהוּדָה וַיֹּאמֶר צָדְקָה מִמֶּנִּי כִּי־עַל־כֵּן לֹא־נְתַתִּיהָ לְשֵׁלָה בְנִי

The word used here, וַיַּכֵּר *(vayaker)*, likewise means recognize. By facing the truth and not running from it, Judah is once again vested with his kingly signet, bracelet, and staff.

He is a true king in his heart. This episode with Tamar prepares Judah to face Joseph later in the story.

Meanwhile, in Egypt, Joseph has miraculously risen to power. His brothers have not fared as well. They travel to Egypt seeking relief from the famine that has gripped their region. They travel as virtual beggars, seeking bread from a foreign land. They do not recognize Joseph. Of course, he recognizes them. He treats them poorly, demanding they bring their youngest brother, Benjamin, knowing the turmoil that will result.

The brothers return to their father and convince Jacob that he must let his most beloved son go. He reluctantly agrees. Jacob does not know that Joseph is alive. So in his mind Benjamin is the only one left. When Benjamin arrives in Egypt, Joseph has his cup planted in the boy's sack and accuses him of theft. He demands that Benjamin remain with him as a slave.

Then Judah gives his now-famous speech to Joseph (Genesis 44:18-34). He tells Joseph that Benjamin is the only brother left alive from his mother, Rachel, admitting that Joseph and Benjamin are the only two sons of Jacob's wife whom Jacob loved most. Judah, a son of Leah, is able to recognize that Jacob favors the sons of Rachel above the sons of Leah. For the first time, he is able to admit (recognize) this truth. Years ago, he suggested that Joseph be sold into slavery. Now Rachel's second son is facing slavery. Judah offers himself in the place of Benjamin:

> "Now therefore, please let your servant remain instead of the lad as a slave to my lord, and let the lad go up with his brothers. For how shall I go up to my father if the lad *is* not with me, lest perhaps I see the evil that would come upon my father?" (Genesis 44:33-34 NKJ)

For the sake of his father, Judah is offering his life for his brother's. Such a dramatic change took place in the heart of this man! His willingness to lay down his life for his brother links him with his descendant, the Messiah Yeshua Himself, who gave His life for his brothers, the Jews, as well as for the entire world. He, like Judah, did it for the sake of His Father. By this selfless act, Judah restores the family. Joseph reveals himself to his brothers right after Judah's speech.

Likewise, Yeshua, the Messiah restores the family of God by dying on the cross for the sins of humanity. It is a character of the true king to give his life for others. And this is why Judah becomes a foundation for the eternal throne. His descendant, Messiah Yeshua, will one day sit on the eternal throne and rule in righteousness with true justice.

What can we learn from the life of Judah? Willingness to recognize the truth and respond accordingly makes us Messiah-like people, who are empowered to advance God's Kingdom. We too are destined to receive the crown, as Yeshua Himself said:

> Be faithful until death, and I will give you the crown of life. (Revelation 2:10b)

Yeshua spoke this to the congregation that was about to experience persecution. Are you willing to be faithful to the truth, regardless of the challenges you are facing?

14
The Elephant Out of Hiding

How will God's Kingdom be established? What are the prophesies we have seen fulfilled in our days?

I live in an Israeli town called Zichron Yaakov. Today it is heavily visited by local tourists. But not many tourists from outside of Israel know about this town or its history.

Zichron Yaakov was founded in 1882, at the beginning of the first Aliyah. The term Aliyah applies to the return of the Jewish people back to the land, which God promised to Abraham. Before 1948 when Israel was established as a nation, there were five waves of Aliyah – five waves of Jewish immigration to the Land of Israel. The first wave of immigration began in 1882 and lasted until 1903. There were twenty-five towns established during this period, and Zichron Yaakov was among the towns that were built first. It sits on the southern part of the Carmel Mountain range.

There are several prophesies in the Bible that were fulfilled in this town. The first one is in the book of the prophet Micah:

> Yet the land shall be desolate because of those who dwell in it, and for the fruit of their deeds. Shepherd Your people with Your staff, the flock of Your heritage, who dwell solitarily in a woodland, *in the midst*

of Carmel; let them feed in Bashan and Gilead, as in days of old. "As in the days when you came out of the land of Egypt, I will show them wonders." (Micah 7:13-15 NKJ)

First the prophet describes desolation. Several prophets declared that the people of Israel would go into exile because of their disobedience and the land would become desolate:

> But I scattered them with a whirlwind among all the nations which they had not known. Thus the land became desolate after them, so that no one passed through or returned; for they made the pleasant land desolate." (Zechariah 7:14 NKJ)

Here Zechariah prophesizes the second exile for the people of Judah, because the first exile took them to only one place -- Babylon. That exile lasted 70 years. But the second exile lasted two thousand years, and the Jewish people were scattered "among all the nations."

The prophets knew people would come back to Carmel, where God would enact miracles like the ones that took place during the exodus from Egypt. The exodus from the last exile, what I call modern day Babylon, began in 1882. People came back, settled on the Carmel Mountain and built Zichron Yaakov, just as Micah prophesied.

Another prophecy in Isaiah 11 says:

> It shall come to pass in that day that the Lord shall set His hand again the second time to recover the remnant of His people who are left, from Assyria and

THE ELEPHANT OUT OF HIDING

Egypt, from Pathros and Cush, from Elam and Shinar, from Hamath and the islands of the sea. He will set up a banner for the nations, and will assemble the outcasts of Israel, and gather together the dispersed of Judah from the four corners of the earth. (Isaiah 11: 11-12 NKJ)

Isaiah here talks about the second return of the Jewish people back to the Land. And as they come back, the banner will be set up for the nations. The Hebrew word for banner here is נֵס *(nes)*, which also means a miracle. God says that the return of the Jewish people back to the land is a miraculous sign to all the nations.

In the center of Zichron Yaakov, on the stone wall, are the words of Ben Gurion quoting his speech when he visited the town:

אלה דברי דוד בן גוריון בביקורו במושבה: כאן קמה המדי־נה. הרבה מושבות ניבנו והרבה אולי אוד ייבנו. אולם מושבות כראשונות לא ייבנו הן אינן נשקלות במאזני כסף וזהב באש יה נבנו בגילוי שכינה.

The last paragraph says:

> This is where the state came into being. Many colonies were built and many may be built. However, colonies like the first ones will not be built. They are not weighed by measurements of silver and gold, but by the fire of Yah they were built with the revelation of Shechinah (Glory).

Though a Socialist, Ben Gurion admitted that a miracle took place. This is what Isaiah and Micah both prophesied:

So, the return of the Jewish people to the Land of Israel is a miraculous sign to all the nations that the process to advance the Kingdom of God has begun. Many Christians still do not see the significance of Israel in the plan of God. But the hidden elephant has begun to come out of hiding.

Jeremiah says:

> "Therefore, behold, *the* days are coming," says the Lord, "that they shall no longer say, 'As the Lord lives who brought up the children of Israel from the land of Egypt,' but, 'As the Lord lives who brought up and led the descendants of the house of Israel from the north country and from all the countries where I had driven them.' And they shall dwell in their own land." (Jeremiah 23:7-9 NKJ)

Jeremiah says that the people will be brought from all the countries where they were driven to, but the emphasis is on the north. The Aliyah began from the north. It started from Romania and Russia. And in the 1970s there was major Aliyah to Israel from the former USSR.

Isaiah mentions that the people of Israel will be brought from the north and also from the south:

> I will say to the north, 'Give them up!' And to the south, 'Do not keep them back!' Bring My sons from afar, and My daughters from the ends of the earth. (Isaiah 43:6)

Not surprisingly, a large Aliyah took place from Ethiopia – south of Israel.

The prophet Zechariah talks about Aliyah from the east and the west:

> Thus says the Lord of hosts: 'Behold, I will save My people from the land of the east and from the land of the west; I will bring them *back,* and they shall dwell in the midst of Jerusalem. They shall be My people And I will be their God, In truth and righteousness.' (Zechariah 8:7-8)

Another important prophecy is that God will restore the ancient northern Kingdom of Israel – the 10 lost tribes will also return home. And some of this has already taken place. Certain people who lived in India were recognized as being from the tribe of Manasseh and were brought to the Land of Israel.

> "I will strengthen the house of Judah, and I will save the house of Joseph. I will bring them back, because I have mercy on them. They shall be as though I had

not cast them aside; for I *am* the Lord their God, and I will hear them." (Zechariah 10:6 NKJ)

So today the Jewish people live in the land promised to them by God. The Aliyah continues. Jerusalem is the capital of Israel. From there the King will reign, and Jerusalem will become the center of God's glory.

Isaiah says this about Jerusalem:

> For Zion's sake I will not hold My peace,
> And for Jerusalem's sake I will not rest,
> Until her righteousness goes forth as brightness,
> And her salvation as a lamp *that* burns. (Isaiah 62:1)

This passage reflects God's heart, which is Jerusalem. God says that He will not hold His peace. The word is לֹא אֶחֱשֶׁה *(lo eheshae)*, which not only means to be quiet but also not stopping an action. Similarly, the Hebrew can be translated, "I will not rest." In Hebrew לֹא אֶשְׁקוֹט *lo eshkot* also means not being quiet. God is saying that He will not stop acting and speaking until righteousness and salvation come to Jerusalem. Can you imagine what God's word can do? And here, God is also looking for our cooperation:

> I have set watchmen on your walls, O Jerusalem;
> They shall never hold their peace day or night.
> You who make mention of the Lord, do not keep silent,
> And give Him no rest till He establishes
> And till He makes Jerusalem a praise in the earth.
> (Isaiah 62:6-7)

THE ELEPHANT OUT OF HIDING

I know people from different parts of the world who are committed to pray for the salvation of Jerusalem.

Before the return of the Messiah, armies from the nations of the world will attack Israel and invade Jerusalem. We see that happening today:

> Behold, the day of the Lord is coming, and your spoil will be divided in your midst. For I will gather all the nations to battle against Jerusalem. The city shall be taken, the houses rifled, and the women ravished. Half of the city shall go into captivity, but the remnant of the people shall not be cut off from the city. (Zechariah 14:1-2 NKJ)

And then the Lord will come. Yeshua said exactly when He will come back:

> "O Jerusalem, Jerusalem, the one who kills the prophets and stones those who are sent to her! How often I wanted to gather your children together, as a hen gathers her chicks under *her* wings, but you were not willing! See! Your house is left to you desolate; for I say to you, you shall see Me no more till you say, 'Blessed *is* He who comes in the name of the Lord!'" (Mathew 23:37-39)

There will be a moment when everything will look hopeless, for all the nations will have turned against Israel. There will only be One who can save them. We have been waiting for Him for centuries. He is our eternal King, the Messiah. Those who are not yet believers will remember the Name that they heard from the believers in Yeshua from different nations, as well as from Jewish believers. And as God pours the Spirit of grace and supplication upon them, they will cry out:

בָּרוּךְ הַבָּא, בְּשֵׁם יְהוָה
Blessed is He who comes in the name of the Lord!

This will be the moment when the nation of Israel will recognize who the Messiah is:

> "And I will pour on the house of David and on the inhabitants of Jerusalem the Spirit of grace and supplication; then they will look on Me whom they pierced. Yes, they will mourn for Him as one mourns for *his* only *son,* and grieve for Him as one grieves for a firstborn. (Zechariah 12:10 NKJ)

Israel will recognize the Messiah who was pierced and died on the cross for their sins. And they will mourn for him. After two thousand years, they will mourn His death.

And the Lord will deliver them from the enemies who are attacking them:

> Then the Lord will go forth and fight against
> those nations,
> As He fights in the day of battle.
> And in that day His feet will stand on the Mount
> of Olives,
> Which faces Jerusalem on the east.
> And the Mount of Olives shall be split in two,
> From east to west,

> *Making* a very large valley;
> Half of the mountain shall move toward the north
> And half of it toward the south.
> (Zechariah 14:3-4 NKJ)

The Lord will come to the mount of Olives and will make His way to the Temple Mountain. There He will be coronated as the King of Israel. From there He will rule over the entire earth. This will be the end of all corrupt governments:

> And the Lord shall be King over all the earth.
> In that day it shall be—
> "The Lord *is* one,"
> And His name one. (Zechariah 14:9 NKJ)

There will be many changes in the world order under the rulership of Messiah the King.

Representatives from different nations will come to Jerusalem to celebrate Sukkoth, known to Christians as the Feast of Tabernacles:

> And it shall come to pass *that* everyone who is left of all the nations which came against Jerusalem shall go up from year to year to worship the King, the Lord of hosts, and to keep the Feast of Tabernacles. (Zechariah 14:16 NKJ)

The level of holiness will be elevated. So that even the bells of the horses, which are unclean animals, and the pots in Jerusalem will be made holy:

> In that day "HOLINESS TO THE LORD" shall be *engraved* on the bells of the horses. The pots in

the Lord's house shall be like the bowls before the altar. Yes, every pot in Jerusalem and Judah shall be holiness to the Lord of hosts. (Zechariah 14:20-21)

What a life this will be under the rulership of King Yeshua. Our perseverance today will allow us to walk in His light, in His truth, and to serve Him with all our hearts and to seek His kingdom. The darkness is getting darker, but the hope of the glorious future that awaits those who love Him makes our endurance worthwhile. With the help of our Lord, we will overcome.

www.ingramcontent.com/pod-product-compliance
Lightning Source LLC
Chambersburg PA
CBHW070109080526
44586CB00013B/1246